RECYCLED SPIRITUALITY

ANCIENT WAYS MADE NEW

Charles Bello

HGM Publishing
a division of Heart of God Ministries
3720 S. Hiwassee Rd., Choctaw, OK 73020

Printed in the United States of America
Published by HGM Publishing
3720 S. Hiwassee Rd.
Choctaw, OK 73020-6128

Cover art and design: Justin Falk. www.justincreates.com

TO LEVI AND JEAN-LUC,

WHO WALKED THE CAMINO DE SANTIAGO DE COMPOSTELA
WITH ME IN THE SUMMER OF 2009.

AUTHOR'S NOTE

Initially, my journey into contemplative prayer was a very personal one, but not one I took alone. I continue to be influenced by a myriad of saints who have preceded me. Their love for God and willingness to document their own movement into prayer made the way much easier for me. These saints span the breadth of Christianity. They include Catholic and Orthodox monks, holiness preachers, Quaker pastors and Evangelical writers. I sat through workshops, spent time in monasteries, spoke with counselors and spiritual directors, and read and reread hundreds of books. I took what I observed and read about and then practiced it on my own. My goal was to understand how God transforms his children from the inside out. I was convinced that God can transform us, and even wants to transform us, but my question was, *What does this look like in real life*? I needed to understand this process, not just so I could pastor others better — I needed it for myself.

As these prayer models have passed from the lives of saints preceding me into my own life, they have been modified and morphed into something that works for me. My goal was never to do the prayer practice perfectly; it has always been to become more Christ-like. But I am a practitioner and equipper at heart. It was only a matter of time before I began training others to do what I was doing.

I want to thank the hundreds of men and women who sat through my workshops, attended my classes and participated in my retreats. It was your enthusiasm and effort to adapt my training to your own life that encouraged me to continue to refine it. Your feedback helped shape this book. In many ways, *Recycled Spirituality* can be seen as a companion to my first book, *Prayer as a Place*, which documents my initial movement toward contemplative prayer. This book is a continuation of that journey as I explore other transforming prayer exercises. It is a little less personal than my first and better approached as a "how-to" manual.

Special thanks to my daughter, Laura Bauer, who read through the original manuscript and did the tedious work of correcting my grammar, and to my editor, Audrey Falk. I cannot think of ever trying to publish anything without Audrey's input.

As always, I am grateful to my wife Dianna. She continues to be my primary sounding board and best friend.

Disciplines for the spiritual life are places in which we meet with Jesus to be taught by him.

DALLAS WILLARD

Christian spirituality should be cultivated in dialogue with godly voices from the past and present.

GLEN G. SCORGIE

CONTENTS

PART 1
RECYCLED SPIRITUALITY

1
RECYCLING SPIRITUALITY

I have come that they may have life, and have it to the full.

Jesus

"Spirituality" wrongly understood or pursued is a major source of human misery and rebellion against God.

Dallas Willard

In the last few decades, spirituality has returned to the radar screen for many people in the Western world. Conventional organized religion is out, but spirituality is in. Those who reject religion are often rejecting a stale system of belief or rules and rituals that have lost meaning for them. Yet there continues to be a hunger for the sacred, for something that gives both meaning and empowerment. What is needed is a faith and spirituality that grounds us in both reality as well as mystery.

The German theologian Dietrich Bonhoeffer possessed that kind of faith and spirituality. Bonhoeffer was imprisoned for his part of the failed 1944 plot to kill Hitler. While in prison he wrote, "I'm still discovering right up to this moment, that it is only by living completely in this world that one learns to have faith.... I mean living unreservedly in life's duties, problems, successes and failures, experiences and perplexities. In doing so we throw ourselves completely into the arms of God." Bonhoeffer was hanged at Flossenburg concentration camp in Bavaria on April 9, 1945, just weeks before the collapse of the Third Reich.

What is required is a spirituality that does not hide us from the evil in the world or take us out of the rough and tumble of life, but one that leads, sustains and empowers us to live a courageous life, where holiness is not just measured in personal piety, but also in justice and sacrifice.

Jesus lived such a life. This Galilean is seen by many Jews as a great man, by many Muslims as not only a great man, but a prophet and a miracle worker as well. For those of us whose mother tongue is Christianity, Jesus is fully God and fully human. He is our Lord and Savior, but not only that, he is our leader. His life and ministry is the template that we are all to use to pattern our own lives.

Jesus came to give us a new way to live so that we can see the burning bushes in the ordinariness of life. Jesus came to give us a new set of values to shape and form us so that we can change the world for the better. Jesus came to give us a new kind of energy. No longer does selfish ambition, fear, shame or bitterness have to drive us, but his abiding presence within empowers us to go the second mile, to turn the other cheek, and at times, at the risk of our reputation and safety, to say no to the dominant culture when it oppresses the weak and takes advantage of the powerless.

We are to follow Christ and learn from those who have followed Christ before us. We are not only to pursue Christ in his teaching and his ministry, we are to follow him in the way in which he lived. It is easy to read just the words of Jesus, marvel at his activities and miss the fact that he, in his humanity, was able to maintain an inner life that sustained and empowered him.

Dallas Willard, in his book *The Spirit of the Disciplines*, writes:

> We can become like Christ by doing one thing—by following him in the overall style of life he chose for himself. If we have faith in Christ,

we must believe that he knew how to live. We can, through faith and grace, become like Christ by practicing the types of activities he engaged in, by arranging our whole lives around the activities he himself practiced in order to remain constantly at home in fellowship of his Father.

What activities did Jesus practice? Such things as solitude and silence, prayer, simple and sacrificial living, intense study and meditation upon God's Word and God's ways, and service to others.

This book examines the ancient ways practiced by Jesus and his disciples throughout church history. These ancient ways help cultivate a healthy interior life that is able to sustain an outwardly Christ-focused lifestyle. The goal is not to become proficient at a particular spiritual discipline; our aim is to be formed from the inside out into the image of Christ. Again Willard writes,

> Disciplines for the spiritual life are places in which we meet Jesus to be taught by him, and he is our guide into how they are best practiced. We should not be overly concerned about how others do them. In a very short time, Jesus will lead us into the practice that is best for us.

This book is not meant to be read from cover to cover in a couple of days. My encouragement is to read a chapter and then take some time to process and practice what you read.

The first section, Recycled Spirituality, is an overview of why we take the time to practice spiritual disciplines. The second section, Ancient Ways Made New, contains more detailed "nuts-and-bolts" instruction about how to practice the spiritual disciplines in a more contemporary manner. With the instruction, I give some historical context as to how the spiritual disciplines have come to us. My intention is to faithfully pass on the essence of what I have received. I have practiced all the disciplines I have written about; some proved more beneficial than others—but I believe that they are all worth investigating.

There are a number of factors that contribute to the effectiveness of a particular spiritual discipline. They include one's temperament, season or stage of life, life circumstances and particular need. We are all in different places, so a spiritual discipline that may not connect with you during one season may be very beneficial at another time in your life.

As the fifteenth-century German mystic Thomas à Kempis wrote in his devotional classic *The Imitation of Christ*,

> All cannot use the same kind of spiritual exercises, but one suits this person, and another that. Different devotions are suited also to the seasons, some being best for the festivals, and others for ordinary days. We find some helpful in temptations, others in peace and quietness. Some things we like to consider when we are sad, and others when we are full of joy in the Lord.

When approaching this book, there are a number of issues that some of us may have to work through.

The first is a mistrust of spiritual disciplines that are outside of our own faith tradition. Many of the practices discussed will seem very Catholic or very Eastern Orthodox. Most of these practices in this book were practiced during the first half of Christian history when there was only one church. Before 1054, the whole church was Catholic or Orthodox. Most of the ancient practices in this book find their origin during this time of our shared history. So you may need to put aside your denominational bigotry.

Richard Lovelace writes in his book *Dynamics of Spiritual Life*,

> In no case does my positive response to any exemplar of Catholic practical mysticism imply blanket theological approval; *it simply recognizes the apparent reality of genuine experience of the Holy Spirit.* (emphasis mine)

The reality of the matter is that someone can have a genuine encounter with God and theologize it poorly (at least in your opinion). As the saying goes, don't throw the baby out with the bath water.

Second, we must be able to practice the spiritual disciplines with theological integrity. You must decide for yourself if the practice of a particular spiritual discipline is theologically consistent within your own Christian tradition. The spiritual disciplines are simply a means to help us connect with God in a more intimate and dynamic way. In the words of Willard, "They are not righteousness, but wisdom."

Third, do not be afraid to fail. Authentic Christian spirituality is not about being really proficient at a particular spiritual practice or achieving goals; it is about experiencing God and being transformed by his Spirit. Failure is a wonderful teacher and an excellent door into the grace of God. Remember, as a follower of Jesus, you are part of a spiritual family totally marinated in grace. You goal is not to do a prayer method perfectly or even "correctly"—your goal is to point your affections toward Christ with the intention of being with God. My encouragement is to practice a spiritual discipline for a few weeks before you evaluate its effectiveness for you in this season of your life.

Fourth, you may be concerned about doing them right. There is a tremendous amount of fluidity in most of the disciplines. Keep your emphasis on God, not on the method. This is sometimes difficult at first. Any time you are learning something new, your focus will naturally be on the mechanics; it is natural to focus on the method on the front end of learning a new skill. So give yourself some slack. In time though, you will want to move past doing it "right" and simply do it in a way that works for you.

Fifth, feel free to morph and modify the exercises to fit your needs and your temperament. Most of the exercises I present in this book have been morphed into something a little different than when they were presented to me. Give yourself permission to experiment and morph them into something that gives you life.

Glen G. Scorgie, in his book *A Little Guide to Christian Spirituality*, says it this way:

The basic dynamics of authentic Christian spirituality will always be the same, but their forms and expressions will be continually new and different. The Spirit is infinitely creative, and we must be open to the fresh and unexpected (though strangely familiar) ways he will graciously meet the next generation.

Sixth, don't over-spiritualize spiritual disciplines. They can be likened to different kinds of exercise equipment one might find at the gym; they are tools to assist you in your spiritual growth. The spiritual disciplines were created by people like us who wanted to grow in their relationship with God. Over the centuries, thousands of disciples have found these tools helpful in developing and maintaining a transforming relationship with Christ. Again, in the words of Willard, "They are not righteousness, but wisdom."

Seventh, don't under-spiritualize spiritual disciplines. There is a reason these disciplines have the word "spiritual" in front of them. It is because the disciplines themselves are not enough to produce transformation. The disciplines are activities we can do in our power that intentionally place us in the transforming presence of God, but ultimately, transformation is the work of the Holy Spirit.

Scorgie writes concerning the Holy Spirit's place in authentic Christian spirituality, "The Spirit's role is crucial, for he is the one who mediates the presence, character and power of the ascended Christ to us. He brings Christ close. So spirituality is about being attentive to the Spirit's voice, open to his transforming impulses, and empowered by his indwelling presence."

Finally, don't be too quick to judge the effectiveness of the spiritual disciplines you are practicing. With many of the spiritual disciplines, the effectiveness is not experienced during the practice, but in the fruit realized afterwards.

A Generous Approach to Tradition

M. Basil Pennington, in his book *Centering Prayer*, shares some insight and wisdom concerning tradition,

> Perhaps you have had the experience—in a class or on a retreat—the group sits in a circle, the leader takes a ball of soft, impressionable clay, holds it firmly for a few moments, allowing the clay to receive the impression of his hands, and then passes the ball on to his neighbor. The neighbor repeats the action, until the ball has made its way around the entire circle. When the last participant finally receives the ball, it possesses the imprint of each one in the circle. Each has made his or her contribution... If no one has dropped the ball, and if the handling on has been careful and concerned, the ball will have retained its original roundness. Nothing of its essential form will have been lost, but its physiognomy will have been enriched by the interesting patterns impressed upon it by the fondling of many hands.
>
> That is what tradition is: a handing on, from one generation to the next, from one person to another, from spiritual father or mother to attentive son or daughter... No matter how loving, how careful the transmitter may be in his receiving and his passing on, if he has truly received the gift in a personal way, in a fully human way, an impression has been made upon it, an enriching one, for it is the impress of a human person, an image of God, the most glorious of created beings.

We are not to be afraid of tradition, nor are we to be a slave to it. Tradition is the passing on of the gifts, insights and experiences from one generation to the next. The outward form of the tradition devoid of the inner essence is a work of futility. Tradition at its worst is legalism that sucks the life out of the practitioner. Tradition at its best is scaffolding that supports an inner life being formed by the grace of God.

CHAPTER 1

The gift of tradition is meant to be received. The essence of tradition is meant to be rediscovered. And if the practice of a tradition helps form you into the image of Christ, it is meant to be recycled.

Un-bundling Tradition

Bundling is the practice of wrapping two or more services or products together in an effort to sell the whole package. For example, a shampoo product might be bundled with hair conditioner or a phone provider might bundle a cable TV service and internet service into a single package. You are free to purchase the whole package or to "un-bundle" them and purchase them separately.

Many of the spiritual disciplines come down to us from previous generations bundled with traditions, theology, value systems, excesses, abuses, and even superstition that may distort the usefulness and the essence of the discipline. An example is the practice of pilgrimages. Annual pilgrimages to Jerusalem were part of the religious world that Jesus lived in. As early as the fourth century, faithful Christians began to make visits to the holy places, especially those sites connected with events in the life of Jesus. Later, pilgrims began to visit Rome, in order to visit the shrines of Peter and Paul and view the many relics of the saints and martyrs that had been collected there.

In time, superstition began to surround the whole practice of making pilgrimages. The pilgrims would venerate the remains of a saint, believing that spiritual or physical healing could result from such devotion. By the time of the Protestant Reformation, it was hard to separate pilgrimages from the abuses and exploitation that surrounded them.

The essence of a pilgrimage is the leaving of one's normal surroundings to travel to a sacred or special destination for the purpose of encountering God. The journey is as much a part of the experience as the destination. If you can un-bundle a pilgrimage from its abuse, you may discover an enriching way to be encountered by God.

Another example is the practice of fasting. Even though fasting has a long tradition in Hebrew and Christian circles, it is not a much-promoted practice in our day. There are even a number of non-Christian faith traditions such as Islam and Hinduism that continue to promote this wonderful practice. To not practice this discipline because other non-Christian groups promote it would be a tragedy.

It works the other way as well. The practice of the labyrinth finds its origins in pre-Christian history. Labyrinth prayer—walking prayerfully and attentively to the center of a serpentine pattern and back out again—was brought into the church, un-bundled from its non-Christian origins and became a tool to help believers slow down, take a "mini-pilgrimage" and focus on their relationship with Christ.

We find the evidence of un-bundling all around us; most of the names of the days of the week and months of the year are all associated with pagan deities. Over time, these names have been secularized and we no longer associate them with pagan spirituality.

It is too easy to discount the benefit of a practice because of the abuses and misuses of it in the past. I encourage you to instead un-bundle the practice from any historical abuses and seek to draw benefit from its essence.

The apostle Paul addressed this process of un-bundling when he spoke of the early Christian practice of purchasing meat at the market place that had previously been dedicated to pagan idols (1 Corinthians 8). His was somewhat of a "don't ask, don't tell" policy. When un-bundling anything that is packaged with theology, values or a history that you are not comfortable with, it must be done thoughtfully, prayerfully, theologically and with personal integrity.

Authentic Christian Spirituality Is an Art Form

Approach spiritual disciplines more as an art form to be expressed and enjoyed rather than a technique to be mastered. Spiritual disciplines are avenues of grace. They are not merit badges of spirituality. Spiritual disciplines are not proof of our holiness; they are the practical means by which we can become holy. We practice them not because we are holy; we practice them in order to become holy. Again, it is not the spiritual discipline that changes us; it only helps us to create a space in our lives to be intentionally present to God for the purpose of being transformed by his grace into the image of Christ.

Judge the Practice by the Fruit

Don't be afraid to approach any of these spiritual disciplines with a healthy amount of skepticism. Authentic Christian spirituality does not require you to check your brains at the door. Judge the spiritual discipline by the fruit it produces in your life. Ask yourself, *Am I becoming more Christ-like? Am I becoming more loving to others? Am I becoming more loving toward myself? Am I more peaceful, more kind, less anxious? Is my love for God increasing?*

If the practices produce the life of Christ within, you can be assured that you are moving in the right direction.

2
ANCIENT WAYS
AS A PLACE OF
TRANSFORMATION

Come to me, all who are weary and burdened, and I will give you rest. Take my yoke upon you and learn from me, for I am gentle and humble in heart, and you will find rest for your souls. For my yoke is easy and my burden is light.

Jesus

Christianity without discipleship is always Christianity without Christ.

Dietrich Bonhoeffer

Why Practice Spiritual Disciplines?

Good question. What spiritual disciplines do is intentionally create a space in your life where you allow God to form your inner life into the nature of Christ. The spiritual discipline does not form you. The spiritual discipline only provides a structure for investing time and energy into your deepening relationship with Christ. Spiritual disciplines provide a place for spiritual formation to take place.

One of the ways Jesus described discipleship was as a yoke. A yoke is used to harness a young ox to a mature, experienced, older ox. The young ox learned to pull the plow or the cart in rhythm with his elder and mentor. Spiritual disciplines yoke us to Christ, providing a place to rest our souls and learn from him. In time we become skilled at following his rhythms of grace.

Jesus shapes our inner life in order to impact a fallen world. Personal piety and rest is always to be coupled with social responsibility and courage. Spiritual activity and ministry can only be sustained by an inner life shaped and transformed by the grace of God. When Jesus called his first disciples to "Follow me and start catching people instead of fish," he was not calling them to a short-term ministry trip; he was calling them to be fishers of men over a lifetime. Outwardly-focused ministry can only be sustained by a transformed inner life.

Jesus also described discipleship as a path or way. Ancient Rome was famous for its well-maintained highway system that connected the far reaches of its vast empire. These highways were used to move both armies and merchandise. Jesus made it clear that the path he leads his followers down is not a broad Roman highway. The path we must travel is a winding, narrow footpath that requires constant awareness. We learn this path by following Jesus. We learn to hear his voice, follow his example and trust in his wisdom. Jesus does more than simply describe the path or dumb it down to a set of rules or principles. Jesus is the path personified.

This path will lead us to love our enemies, pray for those who mistreat us and give to others without calling attention to ourselves. Disciples learn to move in the direction of their leader. This movement must be more than outward compliance. Outward conformity can never be sustained apart from a fundamental inward change.

ANCIENT WAYS AS A PLACE OF TRANSFORMATION

Spiritual disciplines do not produce true Christian transformation. They provide a place to meet with Jesus to be transformed by him. Spiritual disciplines are necessary but not enough to bring about true inner formation. Ultimately, transformation is by the grace of God and the power of the Holy Spirit. The apostle Paul said it this way:

> Work out your salvation with fear and trembling, for *it is God who works in you both to will and act* according to his good purpose. (Philippians 2:12, 13, emphasis mine)

> But *by the grace of God* I am what I am, and his grace to me was not without effect. No, I worked harder than all of them—yet *not I, but the grace of God* that was with me. (1 Corinthians 15:10, emphasis mine)

> So I say, *live by the Spirit*, and you will not gratify the desires of the sinful nature. (Galatians 5:16, emphasis mine)

At its core, a spiritual discipline is to be a synergy of divine power and purpose coupled with our best human effort and intention (whatever it might be at the moment). We can aggressively pursue transformation through certain practices, but we cannot engineer it. Without human effort we will not experience transformation, but neither can we experience it by human effort alone. Paul said it this way in Colossians 1:29, "To this end I labor, *struggling with all his energy*, which so powerfully works in me" (emphasis mine).

There has been a lot that has been written in the last thirty years about spiritual disciplines. Richard Foster's classic book, *Celebration of Discipline,* was groundbreaking for many Evangelicals into the whole concept of how spiritual disciplines can help shape us into the image of Christ.

There are a number of ways to categorize spiritual disciplines. Richard Foster speaks of the inward disciplines of meditation, prayer, fasting and study; the outward disciplines of simplicity, solitude, submission and service; and the corporate disciplines of confession, worship, guidance and celebration.

CHAPTER 2

Dallas Willard, in his book *The Spirit of the Disciplines,* speaks of the disciplines of abstinence and the disciplines of engagement. Disciplines of abstinence are those spiritual disciplines that we choose to embrace in order to deny ourselves of something good for something greater. They also tend to counteract sins of commission, which are those sins we tend to fall into like gossip, pride, greed, lust, gluttony and laziness. The disciplines of abstinence include things such as solitude, silence, fasting, frugality, chastity, secrecy and sacrifice.

Disciplines of engagement help counterbalance the disciplines of abstinence. The disciplines of engagement help us overcome the sins of omission. The sins of omission, generally speaking, are the omission of the good activities we are called to do that get crowded out of our lives because of our busyness or neglect. The disciplines of engagement include study, worship, celebration, service, prayer, fellowship, confession and submission. Willard speaks of abstinence and engagement as the out-breathing and in-breathing of our spiritual lives.

In my own book *Prayer as a Place*, I divide spiritual disciplines into upwardly-focused disciplines, outwardly-focused disciplines and inwardly-focused disciplines. These disciplines yoke us to God, but each moves us in a different direction. The upwardly-focused disciplines move us toward knowing and experiencing God. They include worship, bible study, fixed-hour prayer, liturgical prayer and fasting. We learn to join with the trinity as God loves and worships himself (Luke 10:21). The outwardly-focused disciplines move us toward God's love for others, knowing and serving others as his disciples. Included in this group are intercession, petitioning, prayer for the sick, service, confession and community. The inwardly-focused disciplines move us toward receiving God's love for ourselves. We learn to rest in his acceptance and in that acceptance, find the courage to look at our own darkness, turn away from sin and, by his grace, be transformed. The inward disciplines include solitude, silence, listening prayer, contemplative prayer and journaling.

ANCIENT WAYS AS A PLACE OF TRANSFORMATION

Spiritual disciplines are a place to encounter God. They are less of an activity and more of a place and attitude where we consciously allow ourselves to be in the presence of God.

When writing about spiritual disciplines, Willard says,

> In disciplines we need to be informed and experimental. They are not righteousness, but wisdom. We must be practical with them, and not picky. We must not be "heroic" or think we are earning anything from God. Disciplines for the spiritual life are places in which we meet Jesus to be taught by him, and he is our guide into how they are best practiced. We should not be overly concerned about how others do them. In a very short time, Jesus will lead us into the practice that is best for us.

As you move on to the next section of the book, I want to encourage you to move slowly. Approach the disciplines as fine wine you might sip with a good meal, rather than a soda beverage to be gulped down at a fast-food restaurant. These ancient ways are to be seen as options available, not requirements imposed.

Developing a contemplative prayer life is at the heart of the ancient ways discussed in this book. Contemplative prayer is a way of opening up our hearts so that we can receive God's grace. Spiritual disciplines are not an end unto themselves. God, in his love and care, will take you inward to transform you, but because he loves the world, he will always point you back outward to bring hope and healing to others.

In the words of Scorgie,

> Authentic Christian spirituality is a Spirit-enabled relationship with the triune God that results in openness to others, healing progress toward Christ-likeness, and willing participation in God's purposes in the world.

PART 2
ANCIENT WAYS MADE NEW

3
SABBATH

Sabbath is not dependent upon our readiness to stop. We do not stop when we are finished. We do not stop when we complete our phone calls, finish our project, get through this stack of messages, or get out this report that is due tomorrow. We stop because it is time to stop.

Wayne Muller

The Sabbath is God's gift of rest to mankind. The word "sabbath" comes from the Hebrew word *shabbat*, which means "to cease." It involves a weekly twenty-four hour period of rest and celebration.

The fourth commandment reads: "Remember the Sabbath day by keeping it holy. Six days you shall labor and do all your work, but the seventh day is a Sabbath to the Lord your God. On it you shall not do any work" (Exodus 20:8–10). The Jewish understanding of Sabbath involved a special twenty-four hour rest time once a week that was different than the other six days.

The Hebrew Sabbath began in the evening before the Sabbath, when the family began to set aside the responsibilities of their workweek. Candles were lit, prayers were said, blessings were given, a common meal was shared, and an empty chair was left at the table for the Messiah. The family settled into rest. The next morning, they woke to a new day—a day dedicated to rest, fellowship and the celebration of God's goodness.

Over time, this day of rest, restoration and celebration was turned into a legalistic exercise of Sabbath law-keeping. The enjoyment of God and others was replaced with keeping rules. This approach distorted God's original intention of giving mankind rest from the busyness of life. The Sabbath is both a day and an attitude of rest. It is not enough to have the right practice without the right perspective.

WHAT OTHERS SAY ABOUT CELEBRATING THE SABBATH

Adele Ahlberg Calhoun

Sabbath is God's way of saying, "Stop. Notice your limits. Don't burn out."

Dallas Willard

Sabbath is first achieved in the practice of solitude and silence… The body must be weaned away from its tendencies to always take control, to run the world, to achieve and produce to attain gratification… If we are not rested…the body moves to the center of our focus and makes its presence more strongly felt, and the tendencies of its parts call out more strongly for gratification. The sensual desires and ego demands will have greater power over us through our desperate body and its parts. In addition, our awareness of what it is doing—it is very subtle—and what is happening around us will be less sharp and decisive… Weariness…can make us seek gratification and energy from food or drugs, or from various illicit relationships, or from egoistic postures that are, in Paul's words, "upon the earth." They pull us away from reliance upon God and from living in his power.

Eugene Peterson

An accurate understanding of Sabbath is prerequisite to its practice: It must be understood biblically, not culturally. A widespread misunderstanding of Sabbath trivializes it by designating it a "day off." A "day off" is a bastard Sabbath. Days off are not without benefits, to be sure, but Sabbaths they are not. However beneficial, they're not a true, but a secularized, Sabbath. The motivation is utilitarian: It makes us feel better. Relationships improve. We may even get more done on the six working days. The purpose is to restore strength, increase motivation, and keep performance incentives high.

Sabbath means quit. Stop. Take a break. Cool it. The word itself has nothing devout or holy in it. It's a word about time, denoting our nonuse of it—what we usually call wasting time.

CHAPTER 3

WHAT SCRIPTURE SAYS ABOUT CELEBRATING THE SABBATH

Genesis 2:2, 3

By the seventh day God had finished the work he had been doing; so on the seventh day he rested from all his work. And God blessed the seventh day and made it holy, because on it he rested from all the work of creating that he had done.

Leviticus 16:29, 31

"You must deny yourselves and not do any work—whether native-born or an alien living among you… It is a sabbath of rest, and you must deny yourselves; it is a lasting ordinance."

Mark 2:27, 28

Then he said to them, "The Sabbath was made for man, not man for the Sabbath. So the Son of Man is Lord even of the Sabbath."

Matthew 11:28–30 (MSG)

"Are you tired? Worn out? Burned out on religion? Come to me. Get away with me and you'll recover your life. I'll show you how to take a real rest. Walk with me and work with me—watch how I do it. Learn the unforced rhythms of grace. I won't lay anything heavy or ill-fitting on you. Keep company with me and you'll learn to live freely and lightly."

HOW TO PRACTICE THE SABBATH

1. Plan your Sabbath before Sunday arrives!

2. Make it a family event. Discuss with your family the importance
    of the Sabbath and how you can rearrange your Sabbath for rest,
    celebration and restoration. Ask your children, "How do you
    intentionally leave your school and workweek benind?" Let everyone
    share one thing they would enjoy doing together as a family on
    Sunday. Let everyone share what they would enjoy doing alone on
    Sunday. Discuss what can be done on Saturday to make Sunday less
    stressful. Discuss how it can be a Sabbath for Mom as well as the rest
    of the family.

    A few days after the Sabbath, take some time to debrief and discuss—
    in a nonjudgmental way—what worked and what could have been
    done better.

3. The goal is to develop a kind of easy rhythm that you and your
    family can maintain over a period of time. You must find the balance
    between personal time and family time. This means you must give
    yourself permission to use trial and error to see what works for your
    family.

4. If you are single, your challenge will be a little simpler. This can be a
    day for worship, quiet reflection, rest and doing things you enjoy with
    your friends.

4
SOLITUDE & SILENCE

How can you hear your soul if everyone is talking?

Mary Doria Russell

Solitude is a state of inner stillness that disposes the heart to receive from God. Solitude and silence is not about getting away from people. It is about creating a state of being that enables you to really be fully present with people when you are with them. We have all had the experience of being with someone in body, while our minds and emotions are somewhere else.

Silence is controlling our speech in order to intensify our listening to God. We learn to be quiet first of all on the outside, and then in time, on the inside. By practicing solitude and silence, we are empowered from within to be fully present to God and others. The goal of solitude and silence is transformation, authenticity and empowerment.

Jesus & Solitude

Jesus' public ministry was preceded by forty days of solitude (Matthew 4:1). He was led by the Holy Spirit into the wilderness. During these forty days, Jesus experienced temptation, testing and in the end, empowerment to serve. These forty days of solitude were formative to the ministry of Christ. It was a time for preparation and strengthening for temptation and ministry. His character was tested; ultimately it is our character that carries our ministry.

In the months and years that followed, Jesus would often retire to a solitary place. He experienced these occasions of intentional solitude in the mornings, in the evenings and at times, all night (Mark 6:31, 32; Luke 5:16; 6:12). Before choosing his apostles, Jesus spent an entire night in the hills in solitude, praying to the Father (Luke 6:12). Jesus' disciples not only followed him into ministry, they followed him into solitude as well. "Come with me by yourselves to a quiet place and get some rest" (Mark 6:31).

Following the death of John the Baptist, Jesus "withdrew by boat privately to a solitary place (Matthew 14:13). Before facing the cross, Jesus retreated to a garden with three of his closest friends to be alone with his Father in prayer (Matthew 26:36–39, 42, 44). Solitude was formative to the ministry of Jesus, as it is to those who seek to follow him. The apostle Paul, following his conversion, went into the desert to be alone with God for up to two-and-a-half years (Galatians 1:15–17).

WHAT OTHERS SAY ABOUT SOLITUDE & SILENCE

Dallas Willard

Of all the disciplines of abstinence, solitude is generally the most fundamental in the beginning of the spiritual life, and must be returned to again and again as that life develops.

Henri Nouwen

Solitude is the furnace of transformation. Without solitude we remain victims of our society and continue to be entangled in the illusions of the false self. Jesus himself entered into this furnace. There he was tempted with the three compulsions of the world: to be relevant ("turn stones into loaves"), to be spectacular ("throw yourself down"), and to be powerful ("I will give you all these kingdoms"). There he affirmed God as the only source of his identity ("You must worship the Lord your God and serve him alone"). Solitude is the place of the great struggle and the great encounter—the struggle against the compulsions of the false self, and the encounter with the loving God who offers himself as the substance of the new self.

Richard Foster

To be sure, at first we thought solitude was a way to recharge our batteries in order to enter life's many competitions with new vigor and strength. In time, however, we find that solitude gives us power not to win the rat race but to ignore the rat race altogether. Slowly, we find ourselves letting go of our inner compulsions to acquire more wealth than we need, look more youthful than we are, attain more statues than is wise. In the stillness, our false, busy selves are unmasked and seen for the imposters they truly are.

Dietrich Bonhoeffer

We are so afraid of silence that we chase ourselves from one event to the next in order not to have to spend a moment alone with ourselves, in order not have to look at ourselves in the mirror.

Richard Foster

Simply to refrain from talking, without a heart listening to God, is not silence.

Teresa of Avila

Settle yourself in solitude and you will come upon Him in yourself.

Marcia Ford

But what exactly is solitude… I can tell you what it is not: it's not simply being alone, basking in some much-needed private time. It's not a luxuriously long bubble bath or a stolen hour away from the rest of the household… It's an intense time of isolation from the world and its control.

HOW TO PRACTICE SOLITUDE & SILENCE

Small Steps

1. Find a place where you won't be interrupted. This can be in your car, at a park, along a walking trail or even in the shower.

2. Intentionally place yourself in the presence of God for a set amount of time—five minutes a day is a good start—and acknowledge his abiding presence. "God, I place myself before your presence. Thank you for being with me."

3. If your mind wanders or you start getting bored, quiet your soul by practicing centering prayer, the Jesus Prayer or breath prayers.

4. Simply seek to be present with God for five minutes. You are not looking for an experience or even a word from God. You are simply being present before God with no agenda.

5. When your five minutes are up, thank God for being with you. As you go about your day, reflect on your five minutes: Was it difficult? Was it easy? Was it boring? Did God speak to you or show you anything about him or yourself?

Bigger Steps

1. As your appetite for time with God grows, increase your five minutes a day to fifteen minutes a day. It is better to start small and succeed than to start ambitiously and fail.

2. Set aside a half day to be alone with God. Go to a retreat center, a quiet park, a walking trail. If you have to stay at home, make sure you are alone and the phone is turned off.

3. Take your Bible, prayer journal or nothing but yourself. You can practice extended times of centering prayer, the Jesus Prayer, breath prayers, *lectio divina* or journaling. Give yourself permission to move freely between two or three of these prayer models. If you are outside, you can practice walking meditation as you explore and enjoy with God his creation.

4. Practice listening and being quiet.

5. At the end of your extended solitude time, reflect on what happened during this period of solitude and silence.

5
SCRIPTURE MEMORIZATION

Bible memorization is absolutely fundamental to spiritual formation.

Dallas Willard

Scripture memorization is the process of remembering Scripture passages in order to bring our mind and thoughts into alignment with biblical truth. Committing Scripture to memory is one of the oldest forms of spirituality. Scripture memorization is a spiritual discipline that has fallen into widespread neglect in our day. There is an inherent prejudice in our present culture against "rote" learning—or learning by memory.

The psalmist observed that hiding God's word in his heart was a helpful measure to prevent sinning. Jesus said that the Holy Spirit would take the things he said and bring them to the believer's remembrance. It is difficult to bring something to remembrance if you have not committed it to memory in the first place.

WHAT OTHERS SAY ABOUT SCRIPTURE MEMORIZATION

Dallas Willard

Bible memorization is absolutely fundamental to spiritual formation. If I had to choose between all the disciplines of the spiritual life, I would choose Bible memorization, because it is a fundamental way of filling our minds with what it needs. "This book of the law shall not depart out of your mouth." That's where you need it! How does it get in your mouth? Memorization.

Chuck Swindoll

I know of no other single practice in the Christian life more rewarding, practically speaking, than memorizing Scripture… No other single exercise pays greater spiritual dividends! Your prayer life will be strengthened. Your witnessing will be sharper and much more effective. Your attitudes and outlook will begin to change. Your mind will become alert and observant. Your confidence and assurance will be enhanced. Your faith will be solidified.

Adele Ahlberg Calhoun

Memorizing God's Word allows us to access divinely inspired thought and wisdom. And it works in us even when we are not conscious of its doing so.

WHAT SCRIPTURE SAYS ABOUT SCRIPTURE MEMORIZATION

Psalm 119:9–11

How can a young man keep his way pure? By living according to your word. I seek you with all my heart; do not let me stray from your commands. I have hidden your word in my heart that I might not sin against you.

Colossians 3:16

Let the word of Christ dwell in you richly as you teach and admonish one another with all wisdom, and as you sing psalms, hymns and spiritual songs with gratitude in your hearts to God.

2 Timothy 3:16, 17

All Scripture is God-breathed and is useful for teaching, rebuking, correcting and training in righteousness, so that the man of God may be thoroughly equipped for every good work.

Hebrews 4:12

For the word of God is living and active. Sharper than any double-edged sword, it penetrates even to dividing soul and spirit, joints and marrow; it judges the thoughts and attitudes of the heart.

HOW TO MEMORIZE SCRIPTURE

1. When a portion of the Bible speaks to you, write it on a note card and carry it with you. Pull it out and read it as you go through the day. You may also want to write out the Scripture and tape it to your bathroom mirror, your computer screen, any place you look at frequently during the day. On a daily basis remind yourself of the Scripture until you know it by heart.

2. As you are memorizing the Scripture, let the words sink into your heart. Personalize the verse by morphing the Scripture into a prayer or an affirmation.

3. A good place to start is with classic passages such as the Ten Commandments, the Lord's Prayer, Romans 8 and Romans 12.

4. If you are struggling in a particular area—such as fear, loneliness or forgiveness—memorize Scriptures that address it.

6
SCRIPTURE
MEDITATION

Some read the Bible to learn and some read the Bible to hear from heaven.

Andrew Murray

We ought not to read the Scriptures, but listen to them, for our Beloved is present and speaks to us through them.

Basil Pennington

Scripture meditation is cultivating openness to the Holy Spirit to speak whatever he wishes to speak through the Scriptures. Christian meditation is rooted in the Bible. In fact, the Bible commands us to meditate. In Joshua 1:8, God says to meditate on his word day and night so we will obey it. The psalmist says "his delight is in the law of the Lord, and on his law he meditates day and night" (Psalm 1:2).

In the Old Testament there are two primary Hebrew words for meditation: *haga*, which means to utter, groan, meditate or ponder; and *sihach*, which means to muse, rehearse in one's mind or contemplate. These words can also be translated as dwell, diligently consider and heed. The purpose of

Christian meditation is to have the nature of Christ formed within our souls.

M. Robert Mulholland contrasts reading the Bible for information with meditative reading for spiritual formation. When reading the Bible for information you tend to cover as much material as you can so you can get to the end of the Bible or book. With meditative reading, you keep a "holding pattern" over the words or phrases that speak to you; your goal is not to finish a section, but to meet with God. When reading the Bible for information, you can tend to read in a linear fashion, "moving quickly over the surface of the text." With meditative reading, you read for depth, staying "open to multiple layers of meaning" and deeper dimensions. When reading for information, your hope is to grasp the text and master it; with meditative reading you are allowing the text to master you. With informational reading, the reader controls the text and is looking for what fits into his or her own system of thought. With meditative reading, you are hoping to be shaped by the text; you "stand before the text and wait its address." With informational reading, you approach the words objectively and analytically; with meditative reading, you approach the Word in a humble, detached and receptive way. With informational Bible reading, you are hoping to find solutions to problems; with meditative Bible reading, you maintain openness to mystery and to whatever God may say.

Christian meditation is never to replace careful study of the Bible. All insight and personal revelation must be tested against the plain, main teaching of the Bible. When personal insight contradicts the clear doctrinal or moral teaching of the Bible, you must go with what is biblically true. Christian meditation is best practiced as a supplement to Bible study. Our challenge is to objectively know what the Bible says and to subjectively let it intersect with our daily lives.

WHAT OTHERS SAY ABOUT CHRISTIAN MEDITATION

Jan Johnson

Meditation is taking the time to read a passage slowly and bringing all our mind to the passage in quiet alertness. Instead of analyzing words, we enter into the passage, letting the words be spoken to us by the Holy Spirit to see what impact they will make on us. Meditation usually involves quieting oneself, reading the passage, rereading it, and then shutting our eyes to see what stands out to us today. Then we pray the Scriptures so that we are dialoguing with God. God speaks to us in Scripture so that we are dialoguing with God.

Without personal strategies for connecting with God, our daily agendas tend to become: I must have… I must be… I must achieve… But exercises such as Scripture meditation cultivate the heart and guard it… Having a cultivated heart means that we become more and more inclined to look at life as Jesus did… The Holy Spirit does the cultivating as we choose to meditate on God and God's ways.

Dallas Willard

We withdraw into silence where we prayerfully and steadily focus upon it [Scripture]. In this way its meaning for us can emerge and form as God works in the depths of our heart, mind, and soul. We devote long periods of time to this. Our prayer as we study meditatively is always that God would meet with us and speak specifically to us, for ultimately the Word of God is God speaking.

Rick Warren

Meditation is focused thinking. It takes serious effort. You select a verse and reflect on it over and over in your mind… If you know how to worry, you already know how to meditate… No other habit can do more to transform your life and make you more like Jesus than daily reflection on Scripture… If you look up all the times God speaks about meditation in the Bible, you will be amazed at the benefits He has promised to those who take the time to reflect on His Word throughout the day.

WHAT SCRIPTURE SAYS ABOUT CHRISTIAN MEDITATION

Joshua 1:6–9

"Be strong and courageous, because you will lead these people to inherit the land I swore to their forefathers to give them. Be strong and very courageous. Be careful to obey all the law my servant Moses gave you; do not turn from it to the right or to the left, that you may be successful wherever you go. Do not let this Book of the Law depart from your mouth; meditate on it day and night, so that you may be careful to do everything written in it. Then you will be prosperous and successful. Have I not commanded you? Be strong and courageous. Do not be terrified; do not be discouraged, for the Lord your God will be with you wherever you go."

Proverbs 4:20–23

My son, pay attention to what I say; listen closely to my words. Do not let them out of your sight, keep them within your heart; for they are life to those who find them and health to a man's whole body. Above all else, guard your heart, for it is the wellspring of life.

Psalm 1:1–3

Blessed is the man who does not walk in the counsel of the wicked or stand in the way of sinners or sit in the seat of mockers. But his delight is in the law of the Lord, and on his law he meditates day and night. He is like a tree planted by streams of water, which yields its fruit in season and whose leaf does not wither. Whatever he does prospers.

SCRIPTURE MEDITATION

Psalm 119:8–16

I will obey your decrees; do not utterly forsake me. How can a young man keep his way pure? By living according to your word. I seek you with all my heart; do not let me stray from your commands. I have hidden your word in my heart that I might not sin against you. Praise be to you, O Lord; teach me your decrees. With my lips I recount all the laws that come from your mouth. I rejoice in following your statutes as one rejoices in great riches. I meditate on your precepts and consider your ways. I delight in your decrees; I will not neglect your word.

1 John 2:14

I write to you, fathers, because you have known him who is from the beginning. I write to you, young men, because you are strong, and the word of God lives in you, and you have overcome the evil one.

Hebrews 4:12

For the word of God is living and active. Sharper than any double-edged sword, it penetrates even to dividing soul and spirit, joints and marrow; it judges the thoughts and attitudes of the heart.

Colossians 3:16

Let the word of Christ dwell in you richly as you teach and admonish one another with all wisdom, and as you sing psalms, hymns and spiritual songs with gratitude in your hearts to God.

CHAPTER 6

HOW TO MEDITATE ON SCRIPTURE

Combining Study and Meditation

Studying the historical, linguistic and cultural facts behind the passage, as well as the context, provides clues to what was intended by the writer of the text. Within an accurate textual rendering, we can meditate with more discernment. Then we are more likely to comprehend what God is saying to us at this moment in life.

Personalizing the Text

After reading the text, ask yourself, If this passage had been written to me today, what might God be telling me? If I saw the words of the Bible as a personal letter from God, addressed to me, what might it be saying to me?

Pondering the Text

Let your imagination flow. Think through the implications of what you are reading. Return to the text throughout the day and the week.

Amplifying the Text

Add your own expressions and expansions of the text.

Praying the Text

Jesus prayed Psalm 22:1 on the cross. Did Jesus simply quote this psalm or was this psalm so embedded in his soul that in his point of anguish these words burst forth from his heart?

Lectio Divina

Scripture meditation is at the second stage of lectio divina.

Do It!

Meditation is both a skill and an art that gets easier the more you practice it. Meditation is like everything else: you learn by doing. The way that people meditate varies widely. There is no one right way to meditate. Approach it experimentally; morph different approaches until you find one that works for you. Expect to be surprised by God.

7
LECTIO DIVINA

Prayer is not designed to change God but to change us.

Thomas Keating

Lectio divina (lek-see-o de-vee-na) is an ancient prayer form that, for the first thousand years of church history, was an integral part of the Christian experience. It is a devotional way of reading, meditating on and praying the Scriptures in a manner that enables the word of God to penetrate deeply into our hearts. *Lectio divina* is built on the conviction that the Holy Spirit inspired the Bible and that the Holy Spirit continues to speak to us through the Scriptures. Through *lectio divina*, we can facilitate the word of God richly dwelling in us (Colossians 3:16).

Devotional reading of Scripture finds its roots in the Hebrew tradition. The early church adopted this practice and built on it. This practice began to be known as *lectio divina*, which is Latin for "divine reading." Saint Benedict, one of the early fathers of the monastic movement, set prayer, work and *lectio divina* as the three primary elements that gave rhythm to the daily life of Benedictine monks. Because of their dedication to the Scriptures and the other holy books of early Christianity, Benedictine monasteries were responsible for safeguarding much of the great literature during the Dark Ages. The Benedictines are also responsible for keeping alive the practice of *lectio divina* for the last fifteen hundred years.

Lectio divina was further refined by Guigo II, a monk who lived in France during the twelfth century. In his book, *Scala Claustralium* (The Ladder of Monastics), Guigo writes,

> One day I was engaged in physical work with my hands and I began to think about the spiritual tasks we humans have. While I was thinking, four spiritual steps came to mind: reading (lectio), mediation (meditatio), prayer (oratio), and contemplation (contemplatio). This is the ladder of monastics by which they are lifted up from the earth into heaven. There are only a few distinct steps, but the distance covered is beyond measure and belief since the lower part is fixed on the earth and its top passes through the clouds to lay bare the secrets of heaven.

At one time, *lectio divina* was seen as four interchangeable parts, but after Guigo, the four parts began to be seen as four progressive steps: *lectio*, *meditatio*, *oratio* and *contemplatio*. For the purpose of training and making simple things even simpler, I have renamed the stages as Read, Reflect, Respond and Rest, and I have added a preparatory stage at the beginning, Ready, and an incarnational stage at the end, Return. I have also added journaling as part of the whole process. Journaling is central to integrating the word of God into our lives.

WHAT OTHERS SAY ABOUT LECTIO DIVINA

Eugene Peterson

Lectio divina is a way of life that develops "according to the Scriptures." It is not just a skill that we exercise when we have a Bible open before us but a life congruent with the Word made flesh to which the Scriptures give witness.

Tony Jones

Three activities dominate the life of a Benedictine monk: prayer, work, and lectio divina… Lectio divina is about one thing: developing an intimate relationship with God by praying the scriptures he gave us.

Thomas Keating

Listening to the word of God in Scripture [*lectio divina*] is a traditional way of cultivating friendship with Christ. It is a way of listening to the text of Scripture as if we were in conversation with Christ and He was suggesting the topics of conversation. The daily encounter with Christ and reflection on His word leads beyond mere acquaintanceship to an attitude of friendship, trust, and love. Conversation simplifies and gives way to communing.

WHAT SCRIPTURE SAYS ABOUT LECTIO DIVINA

Hebrews 4:12, 13

For the word of God is living and active. Sharper than any double-edged sword, it penetrates even to dividing soul and spirit, joints and marrow; it judges the thoughts and attitudes of the heart. Nothing in all creation is hidden from God's sight. Everything is uncovered and laid bare before the eyes of him to whom we must give account.

Colossians 3:16

Let the word of Christ dwell in you richly as you teach and admonish one another with all wisdom, and as you sing psalms, hymns and spiritual songs with gratitude in your hearts to God.

HOW TO PRACTICE LECTIO DIVINA

If you are looking for a passage to start with, I would encourage you to begin with passages that are already your favorites and see what else God might want to say. The Psalms are a natural text for *lectio divina*, as well as John's letters and the Sermon on the Mount. Ask God to show you where to start. I have added time limits only as a guide. You are free to adjust the time to fit your schedule and personal rhythm.

1. Ready

(5 minutes)

Make yourself ready by, first of all, finding a quiet place where you will not be disturbed. If your intention is to make this prayer model a regular part of your devotional life, it's helpful to find a time and place that you can come to often. My personal practice is that I usually do *lectio divina* at the beginning of the day, early in the morning before the rest of the family gets up. The place you choose should be comfortable—my favorite is an overstuffed easy chair in my living room. And because *lectio divina* involves having a conversation with God, I find that a cup of good dark coffee often enhances my prayer time. Conversation with God is developed out of an interior calm of resting, waiting and listening.

Once you're comfortable and calm, choose a brief passage of Scripture, no more than a couple of verses. Don't worry about spending too much time on such a small portion of Scripture. Because our intention is spiritual formation, rather than trying to race through as much of the Bible as we can, it is not unusual to spend a week or more with a single passage.

Then seek to be still and quiet—not only on the outside, but take the time to be still on the inside too. Ask God to meet you during this time of prayer, and then reverently turn your attention to the passage you have selected.

2. Read

(5 minutes)

Lectio is Latin for "read." Read the text slowly, letting your awareness rest on each word, savoring it. *Lectio* is reverential reading, listening both in a spirit of silence and awe. You are listening for the still, small voice of God that will speak to you personally—not loudly, but intimately. Many times, I write out the verse to help me focus.

As you read, be aware of any particular word or phrase that draws your attention. Don't worry about whether or not this word is "from God," simply let yourself be drawn into that part of the Scripture. Once you have identified a word or phrase that caught your attention, you are ready to move to the next step.

3. Reflect

(10 minutes)

Meditatio is Latin for "meditation." Meditate on this word or phrase, allowing it to engage you. Use your mind to analyze the word, to define what it means to you. Let the word engage you emotionally— use your imagination. Be aware of any emotions, memories or mental images that arrive within you as a result of your meditation. Begin to write down your thoughts. After you have spent some time fully engaging your mind and emotions in meditation, you are ready to move to the next step.

4. Respond

(10 minutes)

Oratio is Latin for "prayer." During this part, respond to your meditation with prayer. Ask God why this word or phrase caught your attention—what is he trying to say to you? I usually write this question in my journal: *What are you saying to me?* Then I wait for an answer.

Dialogue with God about what you are feeling or hearing. Take time to listen. Don't try to censor what you think you are hearing from him—just go with it. You can go back later and determine if it lines up with Scripture and the character of God. This is a time to simply and honestly talk with God and yourself. It is during this step that transformation begins to take place.

Once you have spent some time dialoguing with God, you are ready for the next step, resting in his love.

5. Rest

(5 minutes)

Contemplatio simply means "contemplation," or wordless, quiet rest in the presence of God. The purpose of contemplation is not to get a word from God or any sort of divine revelation or experience. The purpose is to simply be attentive to the presence of God as he dwells within—to rest in him as he rests in you. There is a real mystery that happens when you sit quietly before God.

In this step, you are not trying to empty your mind. In fact, trying to empty your mind is impossible. What you are doing is focusing all your mental and emotional attention on God.

Because of our culture and lifestyles, many Americans find that resting quietly before God can be a real challenge. For many, this step can be the most difficult and even seem to be a waste of time. If you find yourself struggling with quieting yourself on the inside, you might try using a short breath prayer. The one that I usually use is, "I receive your love." Other times I turn my meditation or dialogue with God into a short breath prayer. For example, if I'm reading the first verse of Psalm 23 and God is speaking to me about trusting him as my shepherd, I would simply turn my meditation into this breath prayer—breathe in, "You are…," breathe out, "…my shepherd."

If this sounds a bit mechanical, it's not. There is something wonderful that happens when you match your breath with prayer. These kinds of prayers help us to stay focused on what God is doing in our lives, as well as enable us to fulfill the apostle Paul's admonition to think about those things that are true, noble, right, pure, lovely, admirable, excellent and praiseworthy (Philippians 4:8).

6. **Return**

(throughout the day)

Return to your meditation throughout the day. The word and Spirit must change us from the inside out. It is important that we are not like the person that the apostle James describes:

> Do not merely listen to the word, and so deceive yourselves. Do what it says. Anyone who listens to the word but does not do what it says is like a man who looks at his face in a mirror and, after looking at himself, goes away and immediately forgets what he looks like. (James 1:22–24)

It is not enough that you hear from God. It is not even enough to pray about it. God's intention is that his word to us changes us into the image of Christ. We take the time to give ourselves to prayer in order to be changed. We want to move from simply doing Christian activity to becoming truly Christ-like.

Keep returning to the passage and your reflections on it throughout the day and throughout the week. Let the word richly dwell within you; let it penetrate your soul and spirit. Be open for God to speak to you about your thoughts and the attitudes of your heart. Your intention must be that of being changed by the word and Spirit of God—we don't change ourselves. In prayer, we create a space where we can be changed. Prayer does not change us—Christian spirituality teaches us that only God can change us.

Doing Lectio Divina with Others

Lectio divina can be practiced in a small group setting, as part of a family's devotional life or as part of a couple's prayer time together.

When practiced in a small group, the facilitator gives a brief explanation of each step, including journaling. He then leads the group through each stage.

During the Read stage, have the participants take turns going around the room, reading the passage out loud a few times. Using different translations helps give the participants more places to hear a word that catches their attention.

During the Reflect and Respond stages, encourage the participants to write out their meditations and prayer dialogue.

After they've responded, invite the participants to read any of their insights that they feel comfortable sharing. The others in the group are free to offer affirmation, but they are not free to offer advice or correction. If what a person shares seems to be unbiblical, the facilitator might ask to speak to that person later in private.

Then, as a group, spend the last five minutes practicing the Rest stage together. This kind of community prayer exercise helps catalyze authenticity.

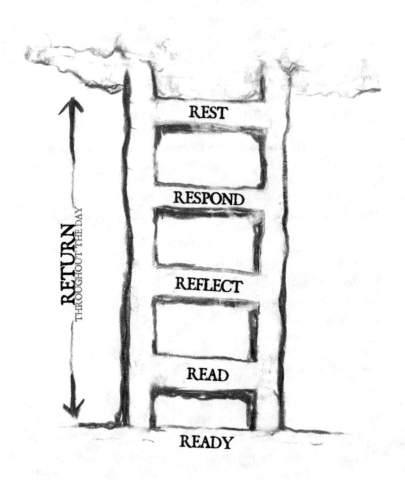

8
CENTERING PRAYER

Prayer is not production-oriented but, rather, the beginning of heaven, the simple enjoyment of God.

Basil Pennington

Centering prayer is a form of wordless, contemplative prayer where the pray-er seeks to quietly rest and be still in the loving presence of God. At first glance, centering prayer looks like something straight out of the New Age movement or the Eastern religions. But centering prayer is distinctively different from Eastern meditation. With those forms of prayer, you attempt to empty your mind of all thoughts. Centering prayer allows for the recognition of thoughts and gently releases them to God. This form of prayer focuses on the awareness of the Holy Spirit residing in the heart of the Christian. The goal of centering prayer is to be attentive to the presence of God within. It is a kind of prayer model few non-Catholic or Eastern Orthodox Christians have been exposed to.

Centering prayer finds its origins with the early Desert Fathers. John Cassian (A.D. 360–430) was born in what is now Romania. He made a twenty-year pilgrimage to the deserts of Egypt to learn about contemplative prayer. Around A.D. 415, he moved to the south of Gaul (France) and established a monastery for men and a second one for women. Cassian was deeply impacted by the Desert Fathers and wrote his book, *The Conferences*, about his conversations with many of the contemplatives he had spent time with.

Taking his lesson from the Desert Fathers, Cassian's focus in prayer was that of inner freedom of the soul, listening to God and being conscious of the indwelling presence of God. He encouraged his monks to repeat a simple prayer: "O, God, come to my assistance; O, Lord, make haste to help me." The purpose of this prayer was to bring the believer to a place of inner stillness before the Lord. He taught that the believer must achieve a state of silence and contemplation, and then God would work in his heart.

Cassian's approach to contemplative prayer was the primary monastic practice for ten centuries in the West; he influenced Saint Benedict, among others. It is the fourth stage of *lectio divina*. However, during the Scholastic period (the twelfth through fifteenth centuries) theologians like Thomas Aquinas recovered the works of Aristotle and other ancient thinkers. Contemplative spirituality began to be discouraged in the church and, in time, was seen as something reserved for the spiritually elite.

WHAT OTHERS SAY ABOUT CENTERING PRAYER

Cynthia Bourgeault

In essence, contemplative prayer is simply wordless, trusting opening of self to the divine presence. Far from being advanced, it is about the simplest form of prayer there is.

Mother Teresa

We need to find God, and He cannot be found in noise and restlessness. God is the friend of silence. See how nature—trees, flowers, grass—grow in silence. See the stars, the moon and sun, how they move in silence…. The more we receive in silent prayer, the more we can give in our active life. We need silence to touch souls.

Richard Foster

Contemplative prayer is the one discipline that can free us from our addiction to words. Progress in intimacy with God means process toward silence.

Adele Ahlberg Calhoun

This prayer may seem mysterious to some because it depends so little on words. We do not give God information about all our needs, projects, ideas, programs, plans and agendas. We don't suggest things we would like him to do. We sit in the presence of God and give him our undivided love and attention.

Because centering prayer is a way of being with Jesus that doesn't cover prayer concerns, some people wonder if it counts as real prayer. Furthermore, if it doesn't make you feel or experience something particular, what does it do?... In centering prayer the goal is to so dwell with Christ that the fruit of this dwelling begins to show up in your life. Centering prayer may "do" nothing for the moment. You sense no rapture, no mystical bliss. But later, as you move out into the busyness of life, you begin to notice that something has shifted. Your quiet center in Christ holds. Centering prayer trusts that being with Jesus brings transformation.

Thomas Keating

Contemplative prayer is a process of interior transformation, a conversation initiated by God and leading, if we consent, to divine union.

WHAT SCRIPTURE SAYS ABOUT CENTERING PRAYER

Psalm 46:10

Be still and know that I am God.

Psalm 62:1

My soul finds rest in God alone; my salvation comes from him.

John 14:23

Jesus replied, "If anyone loves me, he will obey my teaching. My Father will love him, and we will come to him and make our home with him."

Acts 17:28

For in him we live and move and have our being.

CHAPTER 8

HOW TO PRACTICE CENTERING PRAYER

1. As you sit comfortably with your eyes closed, let yourself settle down. Let go of all the thoughts, tensions and sensations you may feel and begin to rest in the love of God who dwells within.

2. Allow the movement of faith and love to well up from your heart, and respond to God's initiative with a short prayer expressing your love, such as "Jesus, you are present with me now; I want to give myself to you." Better yet, let your own prayer come forth and use those spontaneous words.

3. Effortlessly, choose a word or short phrase. This is a symbol of your intention to surrender to God's presence, and let the word be gently present within you. The word or phrase should communicate God's love to you.

4. When you become aware of thoughts or as internal sensations arise, take this as your signal to gently return to the word or phrase, and return to your intention to let go and rest in God's presence.

5. If thoughts subside and you find yourself restfully aware, simply let go of the word or phrase. Just be in the stillness. When thoughts begin to stir again, gently return to the word or phrase. Use your word or phrase as your only response to thoughts, questions or anxieties that arise in your mind.

6. At the end of the prayer time (twenty minutes in the morning and evening is a good balance), take a couple of minutes to come out of the silence—even if you don't feel you need it. Many people find this a perfect time to internally express to God their thanks and to pray for others in need of God's grace. Slowly reciting the Lord's Prayer is another gentle way to come out of the prayer.

The purpose of centering prayer is not to get a word from God or any sort of divine revelation or experience. My usual phrase is, "I receive your love." I then see myself breathing in the love and Spirit of God.

> Again Jesus said, "Peace be with you! As the Father has sent me, I am sending you." And with that he breathed on them and said, "Receive the Holy Spirit." (John 20:21, 22)

The purpose of centering prayer is to simply be attentive to the presence of God as he dwells within, to rest in him as he rests in you.

9
BREATH PRAYERS

Breath prayer reminds us that each breath we are given is God's gift and that God's Spirit is nearer to us than our own breath.

Adele Ahlberg Calhoun

Breath prayer is a form of contemplative prayer that is linked to the rhythms of breathing. The prayers are usually short and seldom, no more than seven or eight syllables. The brevity of the prayer allows you to repeat it over and over throughout the day. When practicing this prayer model, breathe in the first part of the prayer and then breathe out the second part.

The most famous of the breath prayers is the Jesus Prayer: "Lord Jesus Christ, Son of God, have mercy on me, a sinner."

CHAPTER 9

WHAT OTHERS SAY ABOUT BREATH PRAYERS

Thomas the Recluse

Thoughts continue to jostle in your head like mosquitoes. To stop this jostling you must bind the mind with one thought, or the thought of One only. Aid to this is a short prayer, which helps the mind to become simple and useful.

Richard Foster

Breath prayer is discovered more than created. We are asking God to show us his will, his way, his truth for our present need.

Tony Jones

The Jesus prayer has become very significant to me, maybe more than any other practice I've investigated, and it's an important part of my Rule of Life.

WHAT SCRIPTURE SAYS ABOUT BREATH PRAYERS

Genesis 1:7

The Lord God formed the man from the dust of the ground and breathed into his nostrils the breath of life, and the man became a living being.

John 20:21, 22

Again Jesus said, "Peace be with you! As the Father has sent me, I am sending you." And with that he breathed on them and said, "Receive the Holy Spirit."

HOW TO PRACTICE BREATH PRAYERS

1. Choose a brief prayer that is meaningful to you at this season of your life. In time, you may discover that rather than choosing a prayer, a prayer may choose you. A number of years ago, I spent some time at a Benedictine monastery. As I was walking along one of the trails, I began linking my breathing, walking and praying. I started out with, "I receive your love," but what came bubbling out of me was, "I receive your prayers." In the months that followed, God began to teach me how to rest in his prayers for me (Hebrews 7:25).

2. Make yourself comfortable. Breathe deeply, and intentionally place yourself before God. See yourself breathing in the life and love of God.

3. Choose a short, meaningful prayer to breathe. Breathe in the first part of the prayer and breathe out the second part. Match your prayer to your breathing.

   Examples include:

   Breathe in, "Jesus…," breathe out, "…I am yours."

   Breathe in, "Abba…," breathe out, "…Father."

   Breathe in, "Lord…," breathe out, "…I am here."

4. Once you are comfortable with matching your breathing and praying, you can take it outdoors and match it with your walking.

10
THE JESUS PRAYER

Through a pattern of abiding in God that we call contemplative prayer, a change of consciousness takes place. This dynamic sharing of God's nature forms each person and opens them to the mind and very life of Christ, challenging them to be instruments of God's love and energy in the world.

Thomas Keating and friends

The Jesus Prayer is a short prayer consisting of the repeated sentence: "Lord Jesus Christ, Son of God, have mercy on me, a sinner." The goal is that, in time, prayer is not simply something you do, it is who you are.

The history of the Jesus Prayer goes back to the teachings of the early Desert Fathers. Abba Macarius of Egypt (ca. A.D. 300–391) said,

> There is no need to waste time with words. It is enough to hold out your hands and say, "Lord, according to your desire and your wisdom, have mercy." If hard-pressed in the struggle, say, "Lord, save me!" or say, "*Lord*." He knows what is best for us, and will have mercy upon us.

Diadochos of Photiki (A.D. 400–486) taught that inner stillness is gained through repetition of prayer. The Jesus Prayer is foundational to practical Eastern Orthodox spirituality.

The classical form of the Jesus Prayer is,

> Lord Jesus Christ, Son of God, have mercy on me, a sinner.

The actual words of our short prayers can vary. We may say the classic version of the Jesus Prayer, or we might say, "Lord Jesus Christ, have mercy on me." We may say, "Lord Jesus, have mercy."

The words of the Jesus Prayer are based on biblical texts: the cry of the blind man sitting at the side of the road near Jericho: "Jesus, Son of David, have mercy on me!" (Luke 18:38); the ten lepers who called to him, "Jesus, Master, have pity on us!" (Luke 17:13); and the cry for mercy of the publican: "God, have mercy on me, a sinner" (Luke 18:14).

Theophan the Recluse, a nineteenth-century Russian spiritual writer, speaks of three levels in the praying of the Jesus Prayer:

1. It begins as a simple recitation of the Jesus Prayer, sometimes referred to as a prayer of the lips. As one is praying out loud, it is not unusual for the mind to continue to be distracted.

2. In time as one enters more deeply into the prayer, one may begin to pray without internal distraction. Theophan remarks that at this point, "The mind is focused upon the words" of the Prayer, "speaking them as if they were our own."

3. The third and final level is called "the prayer of the heart." At this stage, prayer is no longer something we do but who we are. This level of prayer is seen as a gift of the Holy Spirit and is described as returning to the Father as did the prodigal son (Luke 15:32). The prayer of the heart is also the prayer of adoption, when "God has sent the Spirit of his Son into our hearts, the Spirit that cries 'Abba, Father!'" (Galatians 4:6).

The author of *The Way of the Pilgrim* reported that the Jesus Prayer had two very concrete effects upon his relationship with the world. First, it transfigured his relationship with the material creation around him; the world became a means of communicating God's presence. He writes:

When I prayed in my heart, everything around me seemed delightful and marvelous. The trees, the grass, the birds, the air, the light seemed to be telling me that they existed for man's sake, that they witnessed to the love of God for man, that all things prayed to God and sang his praise.

Second, the Jesus Prayer transfigured his relationship with people. He began to relate to others in a spirit of forgiveness and compassion.

Again I started off on my wanderings. But now I did not walk along as before, filled with care. The invocation of the Name of Jesus gladdened my way. Everybody was kind to me. If anyone harms me I have only to think, "How sweet is the Prayer of Jesus!" and the injury and the anger alike pass away and I forget it all.

What about Jesus' admonition not to not practice meaningless repetition when praying (Matthew 6:7)? The Bible is not against repetition, it is against using prayer as a technique or as a magic formula to garner God's attention and blessings. As you say or think these words, focus on the meaning of the words, praying them from the heart and in the heart.

WHAT OTHERS SAY ABOUT THE JESUS PRAYER

Philimon, a sixth-century monk

Keep watch in your heart; and with watchfulness say in your mind with awe and trembling: "Lord Jesus Christ, have mercy upon me."

Father Callistus and Ignatius

When you will be worthy of this gift of ceaseless prayer in the heart, then, according to Isaac of Syria, you will have reached the summit of all virtues and become a dwelling place of the Holy Spirit; then the prayer will not cease, whether you sit, walk, eat, drink, or do anything else. Even in deep sleep prayer will become active in you without any effort, for even when it is externally silent, it continues secretly to act within.

Anonymous nineteenth-century Russian peasant and author of The Way of the Pilgrim

When the bitter cold pierces me, I begin to say my Prayer more earnestly and I quickly become warm all over. When hunger begins to overcome me, I call more often on the Name of Jesus, and I forget my wish for food. When I fall ill and get rheumatism in my back and legs, I fix my thoughts on the Prayer, and do not notice the pain… I thank God that I now understand the meaning of those words I heard in the Epistle—"Pray without ceasing."

HOW TO PRACTICE THE JESUS PRAYER

1. Make yourself comfortable. Breathe deeply and intentionally place yourself before God. Ask him to come and fill you with his love and Spirit. See yourself breathing in the life and love of God.

2. Breathe in the first part of the prayer: "Lord Jesus Christ, Son of God." Breathe out the second part: "Have mercy on me, a sinner." Match your prayer to your breathing.

3. Once you are comfortable with matching your breathing and praying, you can take it outdoors and match it your walking.

11
THE EXAMEN

We cannot attain the presence of God. We're already totally in the presence of God. What is absent is awareness.

Richard Rohr

The examen is a prayer model for discerning the activity of God in our lives and responding to his loving presence. It is part of a wider body of work by Saint Ignatius (A.D. 1491–1556) called *The Spiritual Exercises*. These exercises were originally written by Ignatius to retreat directors. The examen as it is practiced today is a contemporary adaptation of merely one of the prayer exercises.

God is speaking to us in ways that many of us are unaware of. Paying attention is a learned skill. We must learn to pay attention to God, to our souls, to our physical bodies and to others. The examen is a way to learn how to pay attention to God's activity in our lives and hear what he has to say to us about what we have recently experienced. It is a kind of debriefing that allows you to process your day with God.

The apostle Paul held the strong conviction that God is active in the lives of those who love him and that God is working in all the events of our lives toward forming our inner lives into the likeness of Christ.

> And we *know that in all things God works for the good of those who love him*, who have been called according to his purpose. *For those God foreknew he also predestined to be conformed to the likeness of his Son*, that he might be the firstborn among many brothers. (Romans 8:28, 29, emphasis mine)

The examen is a way to discern God's activity in both the positive and negative forces that come our way.

The examen is basically a daily examination of our deepest feelings and desires. Ignatius called these feelings our consolations—what connects us with God, others and ourselves—and our desolations—what disconnects us. He believed that God speaks to us through our consolations and desolations.

Some of the characteristics of consolations are that they can be encouraging, strengthening, joyful, satisfying, give inner freedom or a sense of vitality—they are life-affirming. Some of the characteristics of desolations are that they leave you feeling discouraged, sad, full of anxiety, trapped or overburdened—they are life-draining.

The genius of this prayer is that you are not simply looking inward. You are asking God to help you review your day, to show you what energized you and what disempowered you, and then to give you his perspective on your consolations and desolations. This interaction can lead to real transformation.

WHAT OTHERS SAY ABOUT THE EXAMEN

Richard Foster

It has two basic aspects, like the two sides of a door. The first is an examen of consciousness through which we discover how God has been present to us throughout the day and how we have responded to his loving presence. The second aspect is an examen of conscience in which we uncover those areas that need cleansing, purifying, and healing.

The Prayer of Examen produces within us the priceless grace of self-knowledge.

Dennis, Sheila and Matthew Linn

The examen makes us aware of the moments that at first we might easily pass by as insignificant, moments that ultimately can give direction for our lives… Insignificant moments when looked at each day become significant because they form a pattern that often points the way to how God wants to give us more life.

As you do the examen, you are listening to both God and yourself, since God speaks within your deepest experience.

Richard Rohr and David Benner

We cannot attain the presence of God. We're already totally in the presence of God. What is absent is awareness. This is the core of the spiritual journey—learning to discern the presence of God, to see what really is… Most of us learn to discern God's presence by first looking for it in the rearview mirror. That is the value of a prayerful review of the day.

WHAT SCRIPTURE SAYS ABOUT THE EXAMEN

Psalm 139:23, 24

Search me, O God, and know my heart; test me and know my anxious thoughts. See if there is any offensive way in me, and lead me in the way everlasting.

Philippians 1:9–11

And this is my prayer: that your love may abound more and more in knowledge and depth of insight, so that you may be able to discern what is best and may be pure and blameless until the day of Christ, filled with the fruit of righteousness that comes through Jesus Christ—to the glory and praise of God.

Philippians 4:8

Finally, brothers, whatever is true, whatever is noble, whatever is right, whatever is pure, whatever is lovely, whatever is admirable—if anything is excellent or praiseworthy—think about such things.

HOW TO PRACTICE THE EXAMEN

To begin, find a place where you can relax and be quiet. Take a few moments to get settled. Acknowledge to God his love for you and his involvement in your life.

Consolations

1. Ask God to bring to your awareness the moment today for which you are most grateful. Ask him to show you how and where he gave you strength, where you felt the most energized, the happiest, the most alive. Sometimes it helps if you go back in your mind to the moment you woke up, and then fast-forward through your day (like you would fast-forward through a video) and ask him to show you your consolation. If more than one consolation comes to mind, choose one to focus on.

2. After you locate the moment or event, step back into it and let yourself relive the joy of that moment. (At the end of each day of creation, God reminds himself that, "It was good.") Thank God for the consolation you experienced. Allow yourself a few moments to enjoy your consolation again; step back into the life-giving emotions you experienced.

3. Ask God then to show you what it was about that event that gave you life. What was said and done that made that moment so life-giving? Sit still and wait for him to respond. If you journal, you might want to write out your dialogue with God. If he does not say anything at this time, simply rest in his love for you.

CHAPTER 11

Desolations

1. Ask God to bring to your awareness the moment today for which you are least grateful, where you experienced sadness, shame, failure, anger, where you felt life and energy being drained.

2. After you locate that moment or event, step back into it and relive the feelings without trying to change or fix it in anyway. Let yourself revisit your pain. It is important that you are honest with your painful emotions. Many of us have been taught to diminish or make light of our pain. This does not benefit us in the long run; it is much more important to be honest with yourself and with God. When I am journaling this exercise, I simply write out what I am feeling, such as, *This makes me so angry, and I feel really humiliated.*

3. Ask God what it was about the desolation that made you so angry, sad, helpless or shameful. Listen to what he has to say. Again, if you journal, you might want to write down your insights and conversation with God.

    Ask God to comfort you and fill you with his love, and sit in silence for a few moments.

Thankfulness

Give thanks for whatever you have experienced during the day. Thank God for being present with you in your consolations and desolations.

12
CHARISMATIC PRAYER

A full life of prayer contains infinite variety. We come before God in liturgical dignity and charismatic jubilee. Both are vital to an unabridged experience of prayer.

Richard Foster

Charismatic prayer is, very simply, the Holy Spirit praying within us. The Holy Spirit creates and sustains this prayer. With this prayer, we have come to the end of ourselves. We try to use words but words fail us. In the language of the apostle Paul,

> The Spirit helps us in our weakness. We do not know what we ought to pray for, but the Spirit himself intercedes for us with groans that words cannot express. And he who searches our hearts knows the mind of the Spirit, because the Spirit intercedes for the saints in accordance with God's will. (Romans 8:26, 27)

Charismatic prayer is not usually thought of as an expression of contemplative prayer, but all true Christian prayer is a combination of the Spirit's grace and our need.

Praying in the Spirit may include, but is not exclusive to, glossolalia or speaking in tongues. A working definition for speaking in tongues is a Spirit-inspired speaking in which the conscious mind plays no part.

It is the speaking of a language—whether known or angelic—which is unlearned by the speaker. Paul again explains that

> Anyone who speaks in a tongue does not speak to men but to God. Indeed, no one understands him; he utters mysteries with his spirit… For if I pray in a tongue, my spirit prays, but my mind is unfruitful. So what shall I do? I will pray with my spirit, but I will also pray with my mind; I will sing with my spirit, but I will also sing with my mind. (1 Corinthians 14:2–15).

Paul's instruction is that we pray with our spirit and with our mind, that we utter mysteries with our spirit and we pray with understanding. This experience is quite common and has been part of the history of the church from the first century to our own. This experience is sometimes referred to as a "prayer language."

Another expression of charismatic prayer is special revelatory impressions and words that the Holy Spirit imparts to the recipient. Many times these words or impressions give the recipient immediate insight into the purposes or the heart of God. Jesus observed that we "live not on bread alone, but on every word that comes from the mouth of God" (Matthew 4:4). When such words truly come from God, they are for the purpose of encouraging us, giving us insight and drawing us nearer to him.

Still another expression of charismatic prayer is sometimes called "resting in the Spirit." It is the experience of encountering the Spirit's manifest presence and power in such a way that the individual is overwhelmed. He may or may not lose consciousness. When this experience is not contrived or manipulated, many report an increase of love, profound inner healing and deeper communion with God.

Charismatic prayer, along with all other kinds of prayer, is neither a mark of maturity nor a badge of honor. It is simply one of many ways that God wants to commune with and empower his children. In the end, all prayer is a work of grace.

WHAT OTHERS SAY ABOUT CHARISMATIC PRAYER

Dr. Martyn Lloyd-Jones

The second danger is that of being satisfied with something very much less than what is offered in Scripture, and the danger of interpreting Scripture by our experience and reducing its teaching to the level of what we know and experience… In other words, certain people by nature are afraid of the supernatural, of the unusual, of disorder. You can be so afraid of disorder…that you become guilty of what the Scriptures call "quenching the Spirit"; and there is no question in my mind that there has been a great deal of this… People are so afraid of what we call enthusiasm, and some are so afraid of fanaticism, that in order to avoid those they go right over to the other side without facing what is offered in the New Testament.

John White

As a conservative evangelical I always called my moments of prophetic insight hunches and intuitions, recognizing only in retrospect and after many years that the insights had in fact resulted from the Spirit's gently coming upon me. In pastoral prayers I would sometimes find myself caught up beyond ordinary prayers as I was momentarily stunned by the vision of what might be. I would be shocked at the bold words I was pouring out. Quickly I would suppress what was happening lest my tongue should run away with me… In my concern for a reputation of sobriety, I had repeatedly quenched the Spirit.

Richard Foster

The charismatic tradition offers an ongoing correction to our impulse to domesticate God. We have a perennial tendency to manage and control the work of the Spirit. We want a nice, tidy God. But as Jesus reminds us, the Spirit blows where he wills (John 3:8).

Carol Wimber

In a dream I was preaching… There was a large crowd. My topic was the gifts of the Holy Spirit. I considered myself an expert on the subject. After all, for years I was responsible for running off members who practiced gifts like tongues, healing or prophecy—gifts I considered dangerous and divisive. I was preaching through my well-rehearsed seven-point sermon when, at the final point, a sensation like hot electricity hit my head, traveled down my body, then up and out my mouth. I was awakened speaking in tongues. I was so troubled by the dream and the experience of speaking in tongues that, like a bag of sand with a hole in it, my confidence and self-assurance drained away. "Perhaps," I thought, "I don't know as much as I thought I did about the Christian life…" "O God," I cried out, "if all that stuff [meaning spiritual gifts such as tongues and healing] is from you, then I have barely known you all these years." There was a long silence. Then I sensed in my heart a gentle answer: "You're right…" Today, I look back on that experience as a "personal meltdown," a breaking of my self-will that was so profound I have never been the same since.

WHAT SCRIPTURE SAYS ABOUT CHARISMATIC PRAYER

Acts 2:4

All of them were filled with the Holy Spirit and began to speak in other tongues as the Spirit enabled them.

1 Corinthians 14:2, 40

For anyone who speaks in a tongue does not speak to men but to God. Indeed, no one understands him; he utters mysteries with his spirit… Therefore, my brothers, be eager to prophesy, and do not forbid speaking in tongues. But everything should be done in a fitting and orderly way.

CHAPTER 12

HOW TO PRACTICE CHARISMATIC PRAYER

There is much talk about the dangers of people seeking experience rather than seeking God, and this is rightly discouraged. But it's been my observation that most people are seeking God *in the experience*. Through an experience with God, they come into a deeper personal knowledge of God's love, receive emotional and physical healing, and are empowered to love others.

I believe that God gives us "dry spells" as well as religious experiences as we follow him over a lifetime. He is God of both the valleys and the mountaintops and everything in between.

1. Ask God to fill you with his Spirit. [All Christians receive the Holy Spirit upon conversion, but the Bible speaks of a continual infilling of his Spirit after conversion (Ephesians 5:18).]

2. Trust that when you ask God for his Spirit, he will not give you a counterfeit. He gives only good gifts to his children (Luke 11:11–13).

3. As you wait on God, if you feel a "bubbling up" of words or syllables that are unfamiliar to you, give expression to these words by speaking them softly. For many, this is how the gift of glossolalia, or speaking in tongues, is first experienced.

4. While in prayer, if you feel a sense of being overwhelmed by God's loving presence, go with it and let it happen. If you think you might fall, find a chair or lay down. Be in a receiving posture; ask God to continue to pour his love into your heart.

13
PRACTICING
THE PRESENCE

We may ignore, but we can nowhere evade, the presence of God. The world is crowded with Him. He walks everywhere incognito.

C.S. Lewis

Practicing the presence is an invitation to see and experience every moment as a gift of God. It is living in the moment, being aware of Christ living within and resting in his love. It involves developing an awareness of God's desire to be active in all your activities, even the mundane and commonplace.

This form of prayer is commonly associated with a sixteenth-century lay brother, Brother Lawrence, a member of a French Carmelite monastery. Brother Lawrence did not have the education to become a cleric, so he spent most of his life cooking meals and scrubbing pots in the kitchen of the monastery, running errands and, in his later years, repairing sandals. He was known for his profound peace and many sought him for guidance. He died at eighty years old in relative obscurity and in perfect joy. The wisdom that he passed on in conversations and in letters would later become the basis for the book, *The Practice of the Presence of God*. The book was compiled after his death. His influence was not only felt by Catholics but he also deeply influenced John Wesley and A.W. Tozer among countless others.

Practicing the presence is more of a personal attitude and perspective than a strategy. It flows out of a desire to live in a deeper awareness of God's activity in our lives. Breath prayers and the Jesus Prayer can help you stay connected moment by moment. The examen operates more like a rearview mirror; it helps you unpack, discern, and listen to God through the things you experienced during the day. Practicing the presence is learning how to "live in the now." It is more about personal relationship than a set of techniques. A life of unbroken relationship is not without effort. Brother Lawrence admits that it took him ten years before he fully entered into practicing the presence of the Lord. On the other side of our effort and desire to be with God is God's enabling grace and unrelenting love for us.

WHAT OTHERS SAY ABOUT PRACTICING THE PRESENCE

Brother Lawrence

I make it my business to rest in His [Christ's] holy presence which I keep myself in by habitual, silent, and secret conversation with God. This often causes in me joys and rapture inwardly, and sometimes also outwardly, so great that I am forced to use means to moderate them, and prevent their appearance to others...

The time of business does not with me differ from the time of prayer; and in the noise and clatter of my kitchen, while several persons are at the same time calling for different things, I possess God in as great tranquility as if I were upon my knees at the blessed sacrament.

Saint Francis de Sales

Several times during the day...ask yourself for a moment if you have your soul in your hands or if some passion or fit of anxiety has robbed you of it... Quietly bring your soul back to the presence of God, subjecting all your affections and desires to the obedience and direction of his divine will.

Thomas Kelly

There is a way of ordering our mental life on more than one level at once. On one level, we may be thinking, discussing, seeing, calculating, meeting all the demands of external affairs. But deep within, behind the scenes, at a profounder level, we may also be in prayer and adoration, song and worship and a gentle receptiveness to divine breathings.

Frank Laubach

This sense of cooperation with God in little things is what so astonishes me, for I never have felt it this way before... My part is to live this hour in continuous inner conversation with God and in perfect responsiveness to his will.

WHAT SCRIPTURE SAYS ABOUT PRACTICING THE PRESENCE

John 15:5

"I am the vine; you are the branches. If a man remains in me and I in him, he will bear much fruit; apart from me you can do nothing."

Philippians 4:12, 13

I know what it is to be in need, and I know what it is to have plenty. I have learned the secret of being content in any and every situation, whether well fed or hungry, whether living in plenty or in want. I can do everything through him who gives me strength.

Colossians 3:3, 4 (MSG)

Your old life is dead. Your new life, which is your real life—even though invisible to spectators—is with Christ in God. He is your life. When Christ (your real life, remember) shows up again on this earth, you'll show up, too—the real you, the glorious you. Meanwhile, be content with obscurity, like Christ.

HOW TO PRACTICE THE PRESENCE

1. Start small by dedicating to the Lord some task you are doing. Talk to him about the task before you start it, continue to speak with him while you are doing it and again when you are finished.

2. Begin the new day by dedicating yourself to practicing the presence during the day. Simply take a few moments at the beginning of the day to ask God to fill you with his Spirit. Throughout the day, continue to ask God to fill you. (God has to keep filling us because we leak.)

3. Throughout the day ask yourself if you are still living out your intention to be in God's presence. Resist the temptation to grade yourself. When you discover that you have strayed from your intention, simply return back to God.

4. Practice fixed-hour prayer. Listen to worship music. Practice breath prayers or the Jesus Prayer throughout the day.

5. Be aware of your emotions and feelings. When you are feeling anxious or angry, let it serve as an invitation to return to the Lord.

14
LABYRINTH PRAYER

The ancient Celts...speak of "thin places," even "thin times"—places and times where the veil between heaven and earth, between the temporal and the eternal, is worn thin.

Krista Tippett

Labyrinth prayer is a contemplative spiritual discipline that involves prayerfully and attentively walking on a serpentine path to the center of the pattern and then back out again. The labyrinth is different than a maze because there are no wrong turns or dead ends; it's simply a means for prayer and meditation.

Pilgrimages have been part of the Hebrew and Christian traditions for thousands of years. As Christianity spread further from Jerusalem and Rome, it became more difficult for Christian pilgrims to make such a long and, many times, dangerous journey.

The labyrinth pattern was adapted by the church as early as the fourth century as a prayer and meditative tool for those who could not make a long pilgrimage. It is a way to pray that involves moving one's feet as well as one's heart.

CHAPTER 14

Though labyrinth prayer is making a resurgence, labyrinths can be difficult to find. You may be able to find one at a retreat center.

WHAT OTHERS SAY ABOUT LABYRINTH PRAYER

Adele Ahlberg Calhoun

Labyrinths are not mazes, nor are they something magical. Walking the labyrinth is not a newfangled technique to jump start your spiritual life. It is a slow, quiet, meditative practice that has historically attended to the desire to make a journey toward God.

Melissa Gayle West

Since the destination is assured, there are no obstacles to overcome, no muddles to figure out, no dead ends to retrace. What remains for the labyrinth walker is simply the deeply meditative and symbolic discipline of setting one foot in front of the other; of honoring the journey itself and what it has to teach. The mind can be stilled and attention paid to the body, the wisdom of the heart, and the graces of being rather than doing.

Jill Greffrion

Two truths about labyrinth praying guided me through my pilgrimage and opened the door to many rich experiences. The first was a deep, intuitional knowing that there was no "right" way to pray the labyrinth. The other was that God is very present in the midst of labyrinth praying.

WHAT SCRIPTURE SAYS ABOUT LABYRINTH PRAYER

Psalm 23:3, 4

He guides me in paths of righteousness for his name's sake. Even though I walk through the valley of the shadow of death, I will fear no evil, for you are with me; your rod and your staff, they comfort me.

CHAPTER 14

HOW TO WALK THE LABYRINTH

1. To begin with, there is no right or wrong way to pray the labyrinth. There is virtually no literature within church history explaining how to facilitate this spiritual discipline. Most of the instructions are recent and are evolving. The primary thing is to not rush the experience and to approach it with an intention to draw near to God.

2. One of the most common ways to pray the labyrinth is to ask God a question upon entering and then to listen for an answer on your way back out.

3. Another method is to pray for yourself on the way in. When you reach the center, stop and pause for a few moments and experience God's love for you. On the way out, pray for others.

4. Some people find it meaningful to recite the Lord's Prayer, the Psalms or breath prayers while walking.

15
PILGRIMAGE

I once walked five hundred miles to attend church.

Arthur Paul Boers

Pilgrimage is a spiritual discipline where the "pilgrim" intentionally leaves his surroundings and travels to a "sacred" destination for the purpose of encountering God. The journey is as much a part of the experience as the destination.

As early as the fourth century, faithful Christians began to make visits to the holy places, especially those sites connected with events in the life of Jesus. Jerusalem was an important destination. Later, pilgrims began to visit the shrines of Peter and Paul in Rome and view the many relics of the saints and martyrs that had been collected there.

In time, superstition began to surround the whole practice of making pilgrimages. The pilgrims would venerate the remains of a saint, believing that spiritual or physical healing could result from such devotion.

There are all sorts of pilgrimages. The destination can be anywhere that has spiritual significance to you. There is the mini-pilgrimage to a favorite cabin in the woods or retreat center. Or a yearly Christian conference or event that you set aside time and effort to attend. There is also the more classical pilgrimage to a historical sacred destination such as Jerusalem, Rome, Iona, Canterbury or Santiago. The challenge is to travel to these places as a pilgrim rather than as a tourist or missionary.

CHAPTER 15

WHAT OTHERS SAY ABOUT MAKING A PILGRIMAGE

Eugene Peterson

Walking could turn out to be the most significant spiritual act in which we will ever engage… Pilgrimage is the ancient practice of walking, usually with others, to a holy site while paying prayerful attention to everything that takes place within and without, soul and body, all the ways that are inherent in the Way, along with the companions who are also on the Way.

Richard R. Gaillardetz

In a postmodern world in which time and space seem compressed and lives of leisure are driven by frenetic consumption, we should not be surprised that many have turned to the medieval practice of pilgrimage as a vital antidote.

Arthur Paul Boers

A pilgrimage is a journey undertaken in the light of a story. A great event has happened; the pilgrim hears the reports and goes in search of evidence, aspiring to be an eyewitness. The pilgrim seeks not only to confirm the experience of others firsthand but to be changed by the experience.

Christian George

Pilgrimage benefits the believer in many ways, but above all it gives us perspective on God, faith and how we encounter both… I have found that the process of pilgrimage is more transformative than simply reaching a destination. Each step of the journey involves deeper communion with

God, and by the end of it, we discover that we have encountered him thousands of times along the way.

Pilgrimage is a discipline for the soul and the sole.

Tony Jones

The point is, mental and spiritual preparation and intention are necessary for a pilgrimage to be a pilgrimage... Pilgrimages are an outward expression of an inward journey.

WHAT SCRIPTURE SAYS ABOUT MAKING A PILGRIMAGE

Psalm 25:4, 5

Show me your ways, O Lord, teach me your paths; guide me in your truth and teach me.

Hebrews 11:13, 14

And they admitted that they were aliens and strangers on earth. People who say such things show that they are looking for a country of their own.

HOW TO TAKE A PILGRIMAGE

1. **Preparation**

   Prepare physically, socially and mentally. Just as an athlete prepares for a sporting event, a pilgrim must do what he can to prepare himself for a pilgrimage.

   If you are going to make an extended walking pilgrimage, it is a good idea to start the practice of daily walking for an hour or so with a backpack before you start your two- or three-week walk to Santiago.

2. **Separation**

   This means leaving home and that which is comfortable. It is not enough to separate physically; you must separate mentally and emotionally. To go on a pilgrimage and take along with you all the comforts of home is to miss the point. You are separating yourself not only from the world, but also unto the Lord.

3. **Exploration**

   Explore God's created world as well as your interior world. The journey is as important as the destination. This is a time you are setting aside to live fully in the present and in the presence of God. The act of making a pilgrimage is an expression of worship in itself.

4. **Reintegration**

   We all have to return home. Resist the pressure to feel that you have to "come away with something." Many times the fruit of the experience is understood long after one returns home.

16
RETREATS

People nowadays take time far more seriously than eternity.

Thomas Kelly

Retreats are specific times set apart for getting away from your familiar surroundings and quietly listening to God and enjoying his presence. The goal is usually to receive refreshing, vision, rest and renewal.

The purpose of a retreat, in the traditional sense, is not to gain more information. It is not for the purpose of getting away to catch up on reading. Retreats are times we pull away in order to get renewed. Take naps and go to bed early. Enter into silence and solitude in the presence of God, who loves you.

It is not unusual for those who live a busy life and are not used to being alone to feel uncomfortable. It may feel like you are wasting time. Many times the benefit of the retreat is experienced after you return back home.

CHAPTER 16

WHAT OTHERS SAY ABOUT RETREATS

Francis de Sales

There is no clock, no matter how good it may be, that doesn't need resetting and rewinding twice a day, once in the morning and once in the evening. In addition, at least once a year it must be taken apart to remove the dirt clogging it, straightened out bent parts, and repaired those worn out. In like manner, every morning and evening a man who really takes care of his heart must rewind it for God's service... Moreover, he must often reflect on his condition in order to reform and examine every piece in detail, that is every affection and passion, in order to repair whatever defects there may be.

Glen G. Scorgie

Jesus accepted the rhythms of human life before God, as he paused to reconnect, be renewed, and regain perspective. We must learn again to be still and attentive. It is a discipline of faith to trust that our needs will be taken care of, even if we pause for a moment and allow the competition to run ahead.

WHAT SCRIPTURE SAYS ABOUT RETREATS

Psalm 23:2, 3

He makes me lie down in green pastures, he leads me beside quiet waters, he restores my soul. He guides me in paths of righteousness for his name's sake.

Matthew 11:28–30

"Come to me, all you who are weary and burdened, and I will give you rest. Take my yoke upon you and learn from me, for I am gentle and humble in heart, and you will find rest for your souls. For my yoke is easy and my burden is light."

HOW TO TAKE A RETREAT

1. Start small by finding a retreat center near you or going out into the wilderness and spending a day away with God. Take your Bible and journal along. Relax. Take a walk. Sleep. Read the Bible. Listen. Don't be in a hurry.

2. During your retreat, have extended times for doing *lectio divina*, practicing centering prayer, contemplative prayer walking.

3. At the end of the year, "harvest" your journal. Read through the last year of your prayer journal and reflect on your spiritual journey during that time. What have you learned? How have you changed? What has God been showing you?

4. Experiment with different kinds of retreats. Spend time in a hermitage. Contact a Catholic retreat center and request to have a spiritual director. Consider having longer retreats of two to forty days.

17
SPIRITUAL JOURNALING

Hearing, I forget. Seeing, I remember. Writing, I understand.

Chinese proverb

Writing is about telling the truth.

Anne Lamott

Spiritual journaling is a form of prayer where you intentionally reflect on and process your experiences in the presence of God. In order to move toward spiritual maturity, you must do more than simply react to pain by striking back or shutting down. It is important that you learn how to use your emotional pain and disappointments as a door into the presence of God. Keeping a spiritual journal is a kind of reflective prayer that enables you to do that.

There is a Chinese proverb that says, "Hearing, I forget. Seeing, I remember. Writing, I understand." This is certainly the case when it comes to keeping a prayer journal. A prayer journal is different than keeping a diary. With a diary, you may simply write about your daily events and musings. With a prayer journal, you are using the activity of writing as a means of prayer and a way to process your inward journey with Christ.

Many of the Psalms are a type of spiritual journal of David's life. They record David's struggles, his pain, his doubts, his disappointments, his insights from God, his victories. In the Psalms, the word "*selah*" is used many times. Though it is often dismissed as a mere musical notation, many commentators agree that *selah* was inserted at points where the singer or psalm reader should pause so listeners could reflect. Take time to read through the Third Psalm. In this psalm, David is working through the pain of his betrayal by his son Absalom. Every few sentences you find the word "*selah*"—pause, reflect.

This section on spiritual journaling uses Psalm 3 as a template.

In the first two verses, David writes about his painful situation and then pauses with "*selah*." In verses three and four, David turns his pain into a prayer; again this was followed by *"selah."* But something really amazing happens during this second *selah*. David's attitude and focus begins to change. It is as if God begins to do something in David's heart.

In verses five through eight, he expresses that he can now find rest; he is experiencing the Lord's strength, fear is gone, and he is asking God to bless his people. This is followed by a final *"selah."* David did not process his pain and disappointments alone; he intentionally and reflectively did so in the presence of God.

Some things to keep in mind when keeping a journal:

Purchase a spiral notebook or diary.

Date your entries.

Keep it personal and private.

Keep it honest.

Write for yourself, not anyone else.

Journal as needed—let it be an easy yoke.

Take time to "harvest" your journals—go back and review what you have written.

WHAT OTHERS SAY ABOUT JOURNALING

Adele Calhoun

In a consumer society it's easy to accumulate experiences, believing the more we have the better! Yet experiences don't necessarily bring wisdom, nor do they automatically transform us. We need to listen and reflect on our experiences in the presence of the Holy Spirit to learn from them. Journaling is a way of paying attention to our lives.

Morton Kelsey

A life which is not recorded and reflected upon is often a life only half lived.

Richard Foster

Journal keeping is a highly intentional reflection on the events of our days. It differs from a diary by its focus on why and wherefore rather than who and what. The external events are springboards for understanding the deeper workings of God in the heart.

WHAT SCRIPTURE SAYS ABOUT JOURNALING

Psalm 25:4

Show me your ways, O Lord, teach me your paths.

Proverbs 7:1–3

My son, keep my words and store up my commands within you. Keep my commands and you will live; guard my teachings as the apple of your eye. Bind them on your fingers; write them on the tablet of your heart.

CHAPTER 17

HOW TO KEEP A SPIRITUAL JOURNAL

1. Write out your concerns with as much emotional honesty as you can muster. I call it "leaning into the pain." Writing helps you to own your disappointments rather than dismissing or diminishing them. Lean into your pain in the presence of God.

    Concerning facing the parts of ourselves we would rather ignore, David Benner writes:

    > To truly know something about yourself, you must accept it. Even things about yourself that you most deeply want to change must first be accepted—even embraced. Self-transformation is always preceded by self-acceptance. And the self that you must accept is the self that you actually and truly are—*before you start your self-improvement projects!*

    > Any hope that you can know yourself without accepting the things about you that you wish were not true is an illusion. Reality must be embraced before it can be changed. Our knowing of ourselves will remain superficial until we are willing to accept ourselves as God accepts us—fully and unconditionally, just as we are.

    After you write about your pain, take a few moments to feel it in the presence of God.

2. Then turn your concerns into a prayer and write them out. Tell God how much pain you are in and ask him for input, grace and comfort. To lean into your pain and not bring it to God will only lead to more despair. It is important to turn your pain into prayer. Ask God to speak to you and comfort you.

    Then with an expectant heart, prayerfully lean into God again and wait on him.

3. As you lean into him, listen. Sometimes an answer may seek to bubble up from your heart. Other times you may sense his love and grace. Other times you will not feel anything at all. Write out your conversation with God.

    Lean into God again, this time with a grateful heart and rest in his provision.

Your purpose is to allow the event you are writing about to be used in the hands of God to transform you into the image of Christ.

18
CONTEMPLATIVE PRAYER WALKING

When through the woods, and forest glades I wander,
And hear the birds sing sweetly in the trees.
When I look down, from lofty mountain grandeur
And see the brook, and feel the gentle breeze.
Then sings my soul, My Saviour God, to Thee,
How great Thou art, How great Thou art.

Carl G. Boberg and R.J. Hughes

Walking could turn out to be the most significant spiritual act in which
we will ever engage.

Eugene Peterson

Contemplative walking is the spiritual discipline of walking with an
intentional awareness that you are walking with God in the midst of his
creation. You have no other agenda except walking with God, enjoying his
creation with him and being fully present to him.

God's creation is his gift to you. God made the world as beautiful as it is to reveal his glory and for us to enjoy. Contemplative prayer walking is simply noticing and taking in the glory of God all around us. Nature is God's first Bible. It is his daily bread for your soul. Just as two lovers might enjoy a sunset or watching for falling stars together, it is the same with God.

Purpose in your heart and mind not to think about the past or worry about the future. Seek to live in the moment and simply walk with God in the midst of his world, enjoying what God enjoys—the birds singing, the butterflies floating on the breeze, the wind rustling through the trees, the warmth of the sun on your skin. Through contemplative walking, look at what you would otherwise overlook. Watch for those things that God sees all the time. Enter into God's joy over his creation and enjoy it with him.

WHAT OTHERS SAY ABOUT CONTEMPLATIVE WALKING

Saint Augustine

Solvitar ambulando—It is solved by walking.

Arthur Paul Boers

We need to expand understandings of spiritual practices. Walking can be one such spiritual practice… I now see that I long ago began meeting God on foot. Walking, I've found, is particularly conducive to prayer. It is not just accidental or circumstantial that Scriptures often speak of this as a metaphor for faithfulness.

Chinese proverb

He who returns from a journey is not the same who left.

WHAT SCRIPTURE SAYS ABOUT CONTEMPLATIVE WALKING

Psalm 19:1–4

The heavens declare the glory of God; the skies proclaim the work of his hands. Day after day they pour forth speech; night after night they display knowledge. There is no speech or language where their voice is not heard. Their voice goes out into all the earth, their words to the ends of the world.

Matthew 6:26–28

Jesus said, "Look at the birds of the air… See how the lilies of the field grow."

HOW TO PRACTICE CONTEMPLATIVE PRAYER WALKING

1. Choose a path through a quiet park, on a walking trail or even in your neighborhood at a time of day when there is not much traffic or noise.

2. As you step on the path, take a few moments to stand still, breathe in the love of God, quiet your soul and dedicate this time to being with God. You have no agenda other than being with God in his creation.

3. Walk slowly, deliberately, being aware of each step. Be aware of your breath, the warmth of the sun, the song of the birds, the breeze on your skin, the rich variety of the beauty around you. All these are gifts from God. Respond with a grateful heart.

4. If you have a difficult time being quiet on the inside, repeat a breath prayer or Scripture verse in your mind. Then coordinate your breathing and walking. I usually pray something like, "I receive your love," or recite Psalm 23 or the Lord's Prayer. You might want to reflect on what God spoke to you through *lectio divina* or journaling and turn your meditation into a short breath prayer.

5. You will discover that there will be times when God whispers in your heart, but most of the time you will simply just walk together.

19
ACCOUNTABILITY
PARTNER

And sometimes—just sometimes, I think—the breakthrough to
authenticity requires that we come out of our comfortable privacy and
confess our sins to others.

Glen G. Scorgie

This is becoming intentionally accountable to another person with whom
you can disclose your stuggles, failures and temptations, a person who
will ask you the hard questions. This can be a more spiritually mature
individual or a reciprocal peer relationship with someone else who
shares your desire to be Christ-like. This is an adaptation of the spiritual
discipline of confession.

In Roman Catholicism, the sacrament of penance, commonly called
confession, is a practice by which people can be freed from their sins
committed after receiving baptism. Catholicism teaches that no one but
God can forgive sins and that God can and does exercise forgiveness
through the Catholic priesthood. God offers forgiveness through the
sacrament of Penance. The intent of this sacrament is to provide healing
for the soul as well as to regain the grace of God, lost by sin. In many

ways, confession and repentance are seen as "religious legal acts" to ensure one's good standing before God.

In Eastern Orthodoxy, confession and repentance have more to do with the spiritual development of the individual rather than the regaining of forgiveness. Sin is not seen as a stain on the soul, but rather a mistake that needs correction.

In general, the Orthodox Christian chooses an individual to trust as his or her spiritual guide. This can be the parish priest or any individual, male or female, who has received permission from a bishop to hear confessions. This person is often referred to as one's spiritual father or mother. Once chosen, the individual turns to their spiritual guide for counsel about his or her spiritual development, confessing sins and asking advice. Eastern Christians tend to confess only to this individual; this creates intimacy and trust with the spiritual director. What is confessed to one's spiritual guide is kept in confidence. Once the confession is made, the one hearing the confession reads the prayers of repentance and asks God to forgive the transgressions committed.

The practice of having an accountability partner draws more from the Eastern Orthodox tradition rather than from Roman Catholicism. At the heart of God is his desire to forgive us and empower us to live in freedom. Accountability partners help us face the truth of our failures and the reality of the forgiveness that Christ offers. They help us live authentic lives and help us process our failures. They give us correction and input within the context of friendship and safety. They can help us think through the events and emotions that preceded our sins. They can also offer prayer and support when we are facing temptations.

WHAT OTHERS SAY ABOUT
ACCOUNTABILITY PARTERS & CONFESSION

Augustine of Hippo

The confession of evil works is the first beginning of good works.

Richard Foster

Confession is so difficult a Discipline for us partly because we view
the believing community as a fellowship of saints before we see it as a
fellowship of sinners. We come to feel that everyone else has advanced so
far into holiness that we are isolated and alone in our sin. We could not
bear to reveal our failures and shortcomings to others… Therefore we hide
ourselves from one another and live in veiled lies and hypocrisy.

Adele Ahlberg Calhoun

The effort we pour into image maintenance separates us from who we
really are. Hiding the "real me" from others sadly hides the "real me" from
me! Image management, pretense—it is a lonely, diseased road.

WHAT SCRIPTURE SAYS ABOUT ACCOUNTABILITY PARTERS & CONFESSION

James 5:16

Therefore confess your sins to each other and pray for each other so that you may be healed. The prayer of a righteous man is powerful and effective.

Galations 6:1, 2

Brothers, if someone is caught in a sin, you who are spiritual should restore him gently. But watch yourself, or you also may be tempted. Carry each other's burdens, and in this way you will fulfill the law of Christ.

Hebrews 3:12, 13

See to it, brothers, that none of you has a sinful, unbelieving heart that turns away from the living God. But encourage one another daily, as long as it is called today, so that none of you may be hardened by sin's deceitfulness.

HOW TO PRACTICE MUTUAL ACCOUNTABILITY

1. Ask God to help you find an accountability partner.

2. When a name comes to mind, approach the person with your desire. Decide how often you will meet together.

3. Begin by sharing your story, your current temptations and areas you would like to grow in. Pray for each other.

4. As you come together in the weeks and months to follow, mutually share your struggles and temptations. Discuss how you can be more proactive. Ask each other hard questions. Covenant to keep confidences.

5. Remember that you are ultimately accountable for your own spiritual health. Your partner is simply an encourager, not an enforcer.

6. If there is a serious problem that continues to trouble you, you may want to consider also seeking out professional help, such as a seasoned Christian, a pastor or even a professional counselor.

20
FASTING

Nothing is more contrary to being a Christian than gluttony.

Saint Benedict

A fast is a self-denial of normal necessities in order to intentionally attend to God in prayer. Fasting is never supposed to be an endurance contest, a competition for spiritual bragging rights or a badge of devotion. The focus must always be on God.

Fasting from food and liquids is the kind of fast indicated in the Bible. Richard Foster describes three kinds of food fasts in *Celebration of Discipline*. A "normal fast" is to abstain from all food and drink except water. A "partial fast" is to limit the food intake to that which is absolutely necessary. And an "absolute fast" is to refrain from all foods and drinking, even of water.

Fasting from food should be done carefully and at times, under the guidance of a physician. Don't fast when you are sick, traveling, pregnant or nursing. It is important to stay hydrated; drink plenty of water. Don't break your fast with a huge meal.

There are other fasts, too. You can fast from TV, shopping, reading gossip magazines, the internet or video games. What you'll soon discover are the compulsions that might be behind many of these activities and the attachment you have to them. Time spent away from these activities might be spent walking, reading the Bible, serving others or practicing solitude.

WHAT OTHERS SAY ABOUT FASTING

Saint Gregory of Sinai

There are three levels of partaking of food: abstinence, adequacy, and satiety. To abstain means to remain a little hungry after eating; to eat adequately means neither to be hungry nor to be weighed down; to be satiated means to be slightly weighed down. But eating beyond satiety is the door to belly-madness, through which lust comes in. But you, firm in the knowledge, choose what is best for you, according to your powers, without overstepping the limits.

John Wesley

Some have exalted religious fasting beyond all Scripture and reason; and others have utterly disregarded it.

Marjorie Thompson

In a more tangible way, visceral way, than any other spiritual discipline, fasting reveals our excessive attachments and the assumptions that lie behind them. Food is necessary to life, but we have made it more necessary than God. How often have we neglected to remember God's presence when we would never consider neglecting to eat! Fasting brings us face to face with how we put the material world ahead of its spiritual source.

Dallas Willard

This discipline teaches us a lot about ourselves very quickly. It will certainly prove humiliating to us, as it reveals to us how much our peace depends on the pleasures of eating.

WHAT SCRIPTURE SAYS ABOUT FASTING

Isaiah 58:5–8

Is this the kind of fast I have chosen, only a day for a man to humble himself? Is it only for bowing one's head like a reed and for lying on sackcloth and ashes? Is that what you call a fast, a day acceptable to the Lord? Is not this the kind of fasting I have chosen: to loose the chains of injustice and untie the cords of the yoke, to set the oppressed free and break every yoke? Is it not to share your food with the hungry and to provide the poor wanderer with shelter—when you see the naked, to clothe him, and not to turn away from your own flesh and blood? Then your light will break forth like the dawn, and your healing will quickly appear; then your righteousness will go before you, and the glory of the Lord will be your rear guard.

Matthew 6:16–18

"When you fast, do not look somber as the hypocrites do, for they disfigure their faces to show men they are fasting. I tell you the truth, they have received their reward in full. But when you fast, put oil on your head and wash your face, so that it will not be obvious to men that you are fasting, but only to your Father, who is unseen; and your Father, who sees what is done in secret, will reward you."

CHAPTER 20

HOW TO PRACTICE FASTING

1. For the novice, fasting should be practiced gradually at the beginning. It would be a good idea to start with a number of "partial fasts."

2. Fast one meal a week. Devote the time you would be eating to worship and prayer. When you feel hungry, communicate this to Jesus in prayer.

3. Once you have mastered one meal a week, try to move onto fasting one whole day a week. Devote your normal meal times to prayer and worship. If you find yourself mindlessly snacking during your fast, simply acknowledge your weakness to God and return to your fast.

21
FIXED-HOUR PRAYER

Orare est laborare, laborare est orare. (To pray is to work, to work is to pray.)

Saint Benedict

Fixed-hour prayer, sometimes called the Daily Office or the Divine Hours, is the regular and consistent pattern of praying at set times throughout the day. Usually these times consist of praying portions of the Scriptures along with Bible reading and prayers that have been passed down through church history.

Along with the Lord's Supper, fixed-hour prayer is considered one of the oldest forms of Christian spirituality. It is surprising that, considering its history and longevity, it is missing from contemporary Christian practice. Jesus and the Jews of his day prayed at set hours of the day. After Jesus' death, his disciples continued to pray this way (Acts 3:1; 10:3, 9, 30). This custom of praying at set hours throughout the day was a part of the early church and has continued up to our day and age.

There has always been some flexiblity with the set times and frequency of the prayer time. In some monastic traditions there are as many as eight times set aside for prayer. Most contemporary expressions consist of three fixed times of prayer: the Morning Office (to be observed some time between 6 and 9 a.m.); the Midday Office (between 11 a.m. and 2 p.m.);

and the Evening Office or Vesper (between 5 and 8 p.m.). These prayer times usually take no more than ten minutes.

There are a number of daily prayer books in circulation including the Roman Catholic *Breviary* and the Anglican and Episcopalian *Book of Common Prayer*. There are also Celtic, Benedictine, Franciscan and Reformed versions. One of the most easily accessible is *The Divine Hours* by Phyllis Tickle. (You can usually borrow a copy at your local library.)

Prayers offered at fixed hours can be spontaneous or liturgical. You can chant the Psalms, pray the Scriptures, pray the Divine Hours, worship with your iPod or simply pour out your heart to God. It can even be a combination of all of the above. The primary thing is that you set aside a regular time for prayer. If you have never practiced a liturgical prayer model, step outside your faith tradition—you might be surprised by what you will discover.

WHAT OTHERS SAY ABOUT FIXED-HOUR PRAYER

Richard Foster

I discovered that regular patterns of devotion form a kind of skeletal structure upon which I can build the muscle and tissue of unceasing prayer. Without this outward structure, my internal heart yearnings for God simply do not hold together. These regular patterns—usually called rituals—are, in fact, God-ordained means of grace.

Phyllis Tickle

Asking me why I keep the Offices is like asking me why I go to church. One, granted, is a place of bricks and mortar, but the other is a chapel of the heart, as powerful a place, albeit of the spirit. The Offices open to me four times a day and call me to remember who owns time and why it is, as a part of creation. All that means really is that four times a day the watchmaker and I have a conversation about the clock and my place as a nano-second in it.

Tony Jones

No matter what my frame of mind as I head to bed, no matter how well or badly things have gone for me on a given day, when I pray this prayer I'm automatically turned outward, to the needs of others, those I know and those I don't. And I'm reminded that in heaven sits a powerful and sovereign God who has all those who need him in the palm of his hand.

WHAT SCRIPTURE SAYS ABOUT FIXED-HOUR PRAYER

Psalm 119:164

Seven times a day I praise you for your righteous laws.

Daniel 6:10

Now when Daniel learned that the decree had been published, he went home to his upstairs room where the windows opened toward Jerusalem. Three times a day he got down on his knees and prayed, giving thanks to God, just as he had done before.

Acts 3:1

One day Peter and John were going up to the temple at the time of prayer—at three in the afternoon.

Acts 10:9

About noon the following day, as they were approaching the city, Peter went up on the roof to pray.

HOW TO PRACTICE FIXED-HOUR PRAYER

1. Choose a regular time during the day when you will stop what you
    are doing, reorient yourself back to God and pray. Don't be afraid to
    start small and just set aside a time once a day to pray this way. You
    may want to start with reading a Psalm or praying the Lord's Prayer.

2. If you want to pray in a more traditional manner, go to your local
    bookstore or library and pick up a daily prayer book. Choose one
    of the prayer times—morning, noon or early evening—or supersize
    things and see if you can pray at all three times.

3. Don't worry if you miss a prayer time. Just seek to get back on track
    when the next prayer time comes around.

4. Before starting your prayer time, take a few moments to quiet
    your heart and mind before God. The focus is not on the prayer
    structure—your focus is being with God.

22
SELF-CARE

The spiritual person puts the care of his soul before all else.

Thomas à Kempis

The body lies right at the center of the spiritual life.

Dallas Willard

Self-care is an attitude and a spiritual discipline that honors God through the proper nurturing and protecting of the body, mind and spirit. It sees life and all our facilities as gifts that we are made stewards of. Self-care involves living a disciplined and joyful life in which you value yourself as God values you.

In Mark 6:30–32, in the midst of the busyness of ministry, the demands being put on Jesus were so intense that he instructed his disciples to "come with me by yourselves to a quiet place and get some rest." This passage gives the reader insight into God's attitude toward work and self-care. Jesus did not reduce life to ceaseless work and ministry.

Self-care is not selfish. It is simply being a good steward of the body God gave you. Our bodies tell us the truth about ourselves. We need to pay attention to our energy levels, addictions to food, sexual tensions, compulsions to work and desires to escape our responsibilities. Human beings were never meant to live and work as though we have no limits. We must learn to respect and honor our mental, emotional and physical limitations. Rest, exercise, time alone, time with friends, healthy food and recreation are the staples of self-care.

WHAT OTHERS SAY ABOUT SELF-CARE

Adele Ahlberg Calhoun

Respecting our bodies (including their limitations) is a way God communicates his council and will to us.

Dallas Willard

The proper retraining and nurturing of the body is absolutely essential to Christ-likeness. The body is not just a physical thing. As it matures, it increasingly takes on the quality of "inner" life… The body increasingly becomes a major part of the hidden source from which our life immediately flows.

Rest, properly taken, gives clarity to the mind. Weariness, by contrast, can make us seek gratification and energy from food or drugs, or from various illicit relationships… They pull us away from reliance upon God and from living in his power.

CHAPTER 22

WHAT SCRIPTURE SAYS ABOUT SELF-CARE

Psalm 139:13–16

For you created my inmost being; you knit me together in my mother's womb. I praise you because I am fearfully and wonderfully made; your works are wonderful, I know that full well. My frame was not hidden from you when I was made in the secret place. When I was woven together in the depths of the earth, your eyes saw my unformed body. All the days ordained for me were written in your book before one of them came to be.

Mark 12:30, 31

"'Love the Lord your God with all your heart and with all your soul and with all your mind and with all your strength.' The second is this: 'Love your neighbor as yourself.' There is no commandment greater than these."

1 Corinthians 3:16, 17

Don't you know that you yourselves are God's temple and that God's Spirit lives in you? If anyone destroys God's temple, God will destroy him; for God's temple is sacred, and you are that temple.

HOW TO PRACTICE SELF-CARE

1. Honor the Sabbath.

2. Develop your own Rule of Life.

3. Exercise and eat sensibly.

4. Get a medical checkup; go to the doctor. Get a mental checkup; go to a counselor.

5. Pay attention. Listen to your body. Pay attention to your sleeping and eating habits. Be aware of your emotions—what is going on?

6. Practice the examen for thirty days straight; record your consolations and desolations. After you prayerfully review your findings, restructure your life around that which gives you life.

23
EXPERIENCING GOD

Those who encounter God, and are changed by him, are never permitted to remain idle. The story cannot end with just relationship and transformation. God's Spirit inevitably stirs such people up to engage in useful service, to find their place in the grand scheme of God's higher purposes.

Glen G. Scorgie

Experiencing God is a method and perspective for becoming aware of God's activity in the world and learning how to partner with him. In partnering with God, the obedient disciple experiences God in a deeper way.

Henry Blackaby, a Baptist minister, wrote a groundbreaking book in 1994 called *Experiencing God*. Though he might be surprised to find himself referenced in a book about spiritual disciplines, his book offers a practical way for a disciple to cultivate an inner life that supports an outwardly-focused, evangelistic lifestyle. Blackaby outlines seven realities that, if embraced, will lead a disciple to a life of experiencing and obeying God. These realities are to be integrated into the belief system of the participants and lived out in faith and obedience.

The seven realities of Experiencing God are:

1. God is always at work around you.

    God did not create the world and then abandon it or leave it to function on its own. God is working in the world. He seeks to work through his people to bring a lost humanity to himself.

2. God pursues a love relationship with you that is real and personal.

    God created us for a love relationship with him. God does not simply want to use you; he wants to share his love with you. This loving relationship is to be a living reality in your life. This means you must take the time to cultivate intimacy with God.

3. God invites you to join with him in his work.

    God is already at work in the world. One of the ways he expresses love to you is by inviting you to partner with him. His desire is to show us what he is doing and then bid us to join with him.

4. God speaks by the Holy Spirit, through the Bible, prayer, circumstances and the church to reveal himself, his purposes and his ways.

    There is no "fool proof" method for discerning God's voice, but God tends to speak to us through his Holy Spirit through at least one of these means. Learn to be attentive to his voice.

5. God's invitation for you to work with him always leads you to a crisis of belief that requires faith and action.

    When God asks you to do something that is beyond your natural ability, you will face a crisis of belief. You will have to decide what you really believe about God. In order to move forward, you must respond with faith-filled action.

6. You must make major adjustments in your life to join God in what he is doing.

   Responding to God's invitation may require you to adjust your thinking, relationships, commitments, activities and even, at times, your beliefs. Many times, to say "yes" to God, you must say "no" to your natural fears and reservations. If God is moving, you cannot stay where you are and follow God at the same time.

7. You come to know God by experience as you obey him and he accomplishes his work through you.

   When you obey God, you experience God's power and presence as his accomplishes his purposes through you. Through your obedience, God reveals himself to you in a way that you would not know any other way. You know God by experience.

The bottom line is that God is at work reconciling the world to himself. Because he loves you as a son or daughter, he wants to include you in his work. He does not simply want to use you; he wants to work with you in the context of a loving relationship. He invites you to partner with him as he reveals his will to you. He requires that you walk in faith and make the necessary adjustments to come alongside him and his purposes. Your obedience leads to a deeper, more heartfelt and experiential knowledge of him.

WHAT SCRIPTURE SAYS ABOUT EXPERIENCING GOD

John 17:3

"Now this is eternal life: that they may know you, the only true God, and Jesus Christ, whom you have sent."

John 5:17–20

"My Father is always at his work to this very day, and I too am working... I tell you the truth, the Son can do only what he sees his Father doing, because whatever the Father does the Son also does. For the Father loves the Son and shows him all he does."

John 12:26

"Whoever serves me must follow me; and where I am, my servant also will be. My Father will honor the one who serves me."

Hebrews 11:6

And without faith it is impossible to please God, because anyone who comes to him must believe that he exists and that he rewards those who earnestly seek him.

HOW TO PRACTICE EXPERIENCING GOD

1. Read Henry Blackaby's book, *Experiencing God*. The challenge will be to actually do the work as instructed and not just read the book!

2. Prayerfully study the seven realities and seek to integrate them into your life. You might try rewriting the realities in your own words and then praying them back to God.

3. Cultivate the second reality ("God pursues a love relationship with me") with regular times of devotion and surrendering of your life and schedule to him.

4. When you go about your day, knowing that the seven realities are true, look for opportunities to respond in faith and trust.

PART 2
RECYCLING THE ANCIENT WAYS

24
DEVELOPING
A RULE OF LIFE

The spiritual life is not something we add onto an already busy life.

Henry Nouwen

A Rule of Life is a personal and regular rhythm that enables the believer to stay grounded in the love of God in order to grow into holiness. A Rule of Life may also take into account personal goals and present needs. A Rule of Life helps establish a pattern for living a balanced life that moves you forward into the purposes of God.

In the fourth century, the early Desert Father Pachomius created a monastic community in Egypt around a Rule of Life consisting of prayer, the Scripture and manual labor. In the years to follow, many numerous religious orders created their own distinctive community rules. In the early sixth century, Saint Benedict of Nursia founded the Benedictine Order in Italy. His Rule of Life became the template for many other monastic communities that followed. His rule continues to be in use to this day. Saint Benedict emphasized balance and gentleness with oneself and with others. He also emphasized the communal nature of spiritual growth.

Benedict wrote that his intention was to

> establish a school for God's service. In drawing up its regulations, we
> hope to set down nothing harsh, nothing burdensome. The good of
> all concerned, however, may prompt us to a little strictness in order to
> amend faults and to safeguard love. Do not be daunted immediately
> by fear and run away from the road that leads to salvation. It is bound
> to be narrow at the outset. But as we progress in the way of life and in
> faith, we shall run on the path of God's commandments, our hearts
> overflowing with the inexpressible delight of love.

When developing a Rule of Life, it is essential that you develop one that
fits you. It should not simply be a comfortable Rule, but one that stretches
you toward God. Some choose to follow a formalized Rule of Life handed
down by tradition. Others choose to shape their own. The important
thing is to have one. Your Rule should be natural, intentional and lived
out in a rhythm that fits your ordinary life.

At the time of the writing of this book, my Rule of Life consists of daily
practicing *lectio divina* with journaling early in the morning. I sometimes
will trade off and simply prayerfully read large portions of Scripture. I try
to practice contemplative prayer walking some time during the day. I also
practice breath prayers and the Jesus Prayer throughout the day, many
times when I am walking, driving or falling asleep.

Once a year, I pause my *lectio divina* and commit an extended time to
doing the examen in order to be made aware of my consolations and
desolations. I also take an extended retreat at a friend's cabin, retreat center
or monastery.

Part of my own Rule of Life consists of my ongoing education and
maintaining good personal health. I walk almost every day and keep a
food diary from time to time. I regularly attend classes and workshops at
local educational institutions and monasteries.

WHAT OTHERS SAY ABOUT DEVELOPING A RULE OF LIFE

Tony Jones

We have lots of options in our ministries, but developing a disciplined spiritual life is not one of them.

Thomas à Kempis

All cannot use the same kind of spiritual exercises, but one suits this person, and another that. Different devotions are suited also to the seasons, some being for the festivals, and others for ordinary days. We find some helpful in temptations, others in peace and quietness. Some things we like to consider when we are sad, and others when we are full of joy in the Lord.

M. Basil Pennington

A rule of life is not so much a thing to be lived as a thing to be lived out. It gives us a supportive structure. Life is a variable thing. It is life, and it goes in all directions… Some days the swift current of life carries us in many directions. We miss sleep and meditation and meals and our exercises. But as the flow slows down again, we fall back upon our rule and move ahead with its support. It channels our energies in the direction we want to go, like the sturdy banks of a watercourse.

WHAT SCRIPTURE SAYS ABOUT DEVELOPING A RULE OF LIFE

Luke 5:15, 16

Yet the news about him spread all the more, so that crowds of people came to hear him and to be healed of their sicknesses. But Jesus often withdrew to lonely places and prayed.

Acts 3:1

One day Peter and John were going up to the temple at the time of prayer—at three in the afternoon.

Philippians 3:17

Join with others in following my example, brothers, and take note of those who live according to the pattern we gave you.

HOW TO DEVELOP YOUR OWN RULE OF LIFE

1. Don't be in a hurry. Take time to practice a number of spiritual disciplines. Pay attention to the practices that seem to give you the most life and draw you toward God.

2. Practice the examen for thirty days and pay attention to your consolations and desolations. Be sure to include your consolations into your life rhythm. It is important to include activities that refresh you and give you life.

3. It is best to start with two or three spiritual disciplines and add to them gradually as you experience some success.

4. As time goes on, and you grow and develop, there is always freedom to modify your Rule of Life to meet your current needs and situation. The important thing is to have a pattern that is doable, sustainable, flexible and profitable. It is to be an easy yoke.

25
CLOSING THOUGHTS ON RECYCLED SPIRITUALITY

For God does speak—now one way, now another—though man does not perceive it... In a dream, in a vision...he may speak in their ears...or a man may be chastened on a bed of pain...an angel on his side...to tell a man what is right for him... God does all these things to a man...that the light of life may shine on him.

Job 33:14–30

All cannot use the same kind of spiritual exercises, but one suits this person, and another that. Different devotions are suited also to the seasons, some being best for the festivals, and others for ordinary days. We find some helpful in temptations, others in peace and quietness. Some things we like to consider when we are sad, and others when we are full of joy in the Lord.

Thomas à Kempis

Moses saw that though the bush was on fire it did not burn up. So Moses thought, "I will go over and see this strange sight—why the bush does not burn up." When the Lord saw that he had gone over to look, God called to him from the bush.

Exodus 3:2–4

The world is ablaze with burning bushes. They are all around us. A brilliant sunset, your daily experiences—both sorrowful and pleasant—the Bible, silence, a comforting touch on the shoulder, encouraging words from a friend, disapproval from a critic, the desperate cry from a stranger—all these things can be ablaze with the presence of God. What is lacking is our awareness. Practicing the ancient ways makes you more alive, more aware.

START WITH WHERE YOU ARE NOW

Spiritual disciplines must be adopted into the life you are presently living, not the one you want. Life circumstances play a large part in what you can presently do. The last thing most of us need is to add another activity to an already busy schedule.

Richard Foster writes, "God intended the Disciplines of the spiritual life to be for ordinary human beings: people who have jobs, who care for children, who wash dishes and mow lawns."

A young mother with a house full of active children may long for solitude but life circumstances restrict her ability to include this spiritual discipline in her hectic life. This may require her to focus on practicing the presence in the midst of her service to her family. Many of the present activities we are all involved in are pregnant with the presence of God. The busy mother or father may need to morph a discipline in order to share it with the family. Contemplative walking can be adapted to be done with small children; so can the examen. *Lectio divina* is great with teenagers. If the busy mother's hunger for solitude persists, then she must ask God to show her how to find the time. Perhaps a neighbor, relative or babysitting co-op can give her the time she needs.

START WITH WHAT YOU ALREADY ENJOY

Religious systems tend to give people spiritual "to do" lists. We are told to pray more, serve more, give more, work more, read more, repent more, attend more, until there isn't any more time or energy left (and then we are told to rest more). To add spiritual disciplines to this list of more things to do would be disastrous. In order to add something, something else must be subtracted. Spiritual disciplines are to liberate us, not put us in more bondage.

There is a good chance that there are things you are already doing that can be channels of grace. I have always enjoyed walking in nature. When I realized that God also loves nature, I began walking, not to get away from people, but to practice solitude and get away with God. I took an activity I already enjoyed and added a "spiritual component" to it. I think fishing and perhaps golf could also qualify.

I also enjoy grinding fresh coffee beans, pouring bubbling hot water into a French press and letting it simmer a few moments. I do this early in the morning before the rest of the family wakes up. This small liturgical act gives me a chance to ease into the morning, give thanks for this legalized stimulant and ask God for grace to start the new day.

I also enjoy making breakfast for my wife and serving her as if she were Christ. (She is his sister!) This act of serving breakfast to my wife has been a place where I have experienced the transforming power of Christ. *Do I continue to serve her if she does not express a sufficient amount of gratitude? Do I want to get something in return for my service? Am I being co-dependent?* These are issues I have had to work through within this simple act of kindness shown to my wife. In the end, it simply boiled down to me showing love to my wife in a practical way.

What are you already doing that with a little adjustment and perspective can be avenues of grace and transformation?

START SMALL & EXPERIMENT

If you are going to incorporate a new spiritual discipline into your life, then start small. Don't be concerned about doing it perfectly. I know that for some personality types, this is a difficult concept to live out. My personality type lends itself to experimentation and I tend to push the boundaries in the name of discovery and innovation.

The ancient way has to become your own. The way you practice it may look different from the way I teach it or others approach it. So what? Give yourself permission to experiment and take the time to find out what works best for you. Allow different kinds of spiritual disciplines, prayer models and even "secular" activity to morph into something that uniquely fits you and gives you life. The purpose of all this is to create a space in your life where you can encounter God so he can form you into the nature of Christ. In the end, you are not graded on how well you performed a spiritual discipline; you will be graded on how well you love!

Again to echo the words of Willard:

> Disciplines for the spiritual life are places in which we meet Jesus to be taught by him, and he is our guide into how they are best practiced. *We should not be overly concerned about how others do them. In a very short time, Jesus will lead us into the practice that is best for us.*

Ancient ways are spaces in our lives where we intentionally allow God to form us from the inside out. They are not self-improvement techniques. The goal is always to be more Christ-like. Remember, the spiritual discipline does not form you; transformation is always a work of grace. The spiritual discipline only provides structure for spiritual formation to take place.

With the spiritual disciplines we need to be knowledgeable of what has worked for the saints that have gone before us. There is tremendous insight and wisdom to be gained from their experiences.

With the spiritual disciplines we need to give ourselves permission to experiment. If a particular model does not connect with you, then let it go. If you feel that your spiritual life has become stagnant, then this is an indication there needs to be some kind of change.

Your goal with any spiritual discipline is to meet with Jesus in order to be transformed into his likeness. You are seeking to connect your inner motives and needs with God. As long as a spiritual discipline is moving you in that direction, it is accomplishing its purpose. Ultimately, Jesus is the one who will lead you into the practice that is best for you. We all have different temperaments and different life situations. He is your best teacher and guide as to how to best practice a spiritual discipline.

THE IMPORTANCE OF A RULE OF LIFE

We need a pattern of spiritual disciplines that provides structure and direction for our growth into wholeness and holiness. To echo again the words of Bonhoeffer, "Christianity without discipleship is always Christianity without Christ." The movement toward maturity and Christ-likeness is a process. You may experience the joy of revival and even have dramatic encounters with God. As wonderful as these experiences are, they don't replace the need for slow, steady movement toward God. We all need a plan for carrying out our decision to becoming more like Christ. We must develop a track to run on.

Willard says it this way:

> The crucial thing is that, as disciples, we have a plan for carrying out the decision we have made to devote ourselves to becoming like our Master and Lord—to increasingly living in the character and power of Christ. Disciples are those who, seriously intending to become like Jesus from the inside out, systematically and progressively rearrange their affairs to that end, under the guidance of the Word and the Spirit.

CHAPTER 25

STAY ROOTED IN CHRISTIAN COMMUNITY

Christianity is a team sport. It is more like soccer than golf. All writers on the spiritual life warn of going it alone. Traditionally, when pursuing a contemplative prayer life, people are encouraged to find a spiritual director. For most people, this will not happen. There are a number of reasons for this. First of all, there are limited numbers of people who have been trained as spiritual directors (though the numbers are growing). Second, for many Christians this means stepping outside their faith tradition and this can be very difficult and unsettling for many people.

In his book, *Satisfy Your Soul*, Bruce Demarest provides a great tool to help us understand the different ways we can wrap community around our contemplative prayer experience. In my own book, *Prayer as A Place*, I have adapted his outline and added some insights of my own. They are worth repeating. As you read through the suggestions, I move from a very informal, unstructured and sometimes reciprocal relationship to a more formal, structured, one-directional relationship.

Books on the Spiritual Life

Do not underestimate the value of those who have traveled this path before you. There is real benefit in reading the journey of others while processing your own. You don't have to agree with everything they write, but there is wisdom to be found as you read how they processed their own journey.

Spiritual Friend

Finding others on a similar journey is a great benefit. Spiritual friends can be two or more Christians—who are on a relatively equal basis—who support, encourage and pray for one another. Having others you can share insights with is a tremendous blessing. This friendship can be as intimate as a husband and wife doing spiritual formation together. Because of the level of intimacy, if you choose a spiritual friend other than your spouse, I would caution you to take the necessary steps to protect your marriage. For me this would exclude anyone of the opposite sex.

Spiritual Guidance

This is another informal helping ministry. It includes coming alongside a friend and talking about difficult issues, recommending a book, etc. This person can be a pastor or simply an older or more mature Christian.

Spiritual Formation Group

This is a group of Christians who get together on a regular basis to practice a spiritual discipline or discuss spiritual and personal issues. There is a sense of mutual accountability and self-disclosure. The group may or may not have a designated leader. Early in my development of my own contemplative prayer life, these kinds of groups were invaluable.

Spiritual Mentoring

This is a more formal relationship in which a mature Christian offers another believer regular instruction, training and modeling in spiritual formation and ministry. This is someone who has taken the journey and is willing to share his or her wisdom and insight with you.

Spiritual Director

This is a structured ministry in which a gifted and experienced Christian helps another believer grow in relationship and obedience to Christ. The spiritual director is usually gifted in discernment, wisdom and knowledge; in fact, many see that the role of a spiritual director is a gift given by the Holy Spirit. Their task is to help people process their relationship with Christ. This is a specialized ministry, and if you are seeing a spiritual director, some kind of financial compensation should be offered. Different traditions have different policies concerning compensation. Some religious communities forbid their spiritual directors to receive pay. Others will suggest that you make a donation to the retreat center or religious community. Some directors are self-employed; in this case, your compensation would be given directly to the individual.

Most of the ancient ways come down to us from a Christian culture that understood and embraced community. Spiritual disciplines are meant to be practiced in the context of mutual submission and committed relationship. Transforming deep-seated behavior patterns rooted in fear and sin takes a lot of energy and discipline. In the words of the apostle Paul, "To this end I labor, struggling with all his energy, which so powerfully works in me" (Colossians 1:9).

Ultimately, the application of any spiritual discipline is up to the individual, but having people who love you and are willing to walk alongside you is often the difference between success and failure. Recycled spirituality is about cultivating an inner life with Christ that will sustain you as you join with Christ in his mission in the world.

> "Are you tired? Worn out? Burned out on religion? Come to me. Get away with me and you'll recover your life. I'll show you how to take a real rest. Walk with me and work with me—watch how I do it. Learn the unforced rhythms of grace. I won't lay anything heavy or ill-fitting on you. Keep company with me and you'll learn to live freely and lightly." (Matthew 11:28–30, MSG)

THE ROAD BACK INTO ACTIVITY

The ancient ways are not an end unto themselves. God, in his love and care, will take you inward to transform you, but because he loves the world, he will always point you back outward to bring hope and healing to others. The work of inner transformation finds its completion when we embrace self-denial and join with Christ in his mission in the world. God wants to dwell in us and work through us.

> For we are God's handiwork, created in Christ Jesus to do good works, which God prepared in advance for us to do. (Ephesians 2:10)

We are all called to contribute to the advance of God's kingdom.

SELECTED BIBLIOGRAPHY

Bello, Charles. *Prayer as a Place: Spirituality that Transforms* (HGM Publishing, 2008).

Blackaby, Henry T. and Claude V. King. *Experiencing God: How to Live the Full Adventure of Knowing and Doing the Will of God* (Broadman & Holman Publishers, 1994).

Bourgeault, Cynthia. *Centering Prayer and Inner Awakening* (Cowley Publications, 2004).

Calhoun, Adele Ahlberg. *Spiritual Disciplines Handbook: Practices That Transform Us* (InterVarsity Press, 2005).

Davids, Judy. Pastor's Sabbath Retreat (September 21–October 1, 2004; September 11–22, 2007).

Demarest, Dr. Bruce. *Satisfy Your Soul: Restoring the Heart of Christian Spirituality* (NavPress, 1999).

Demarest, Dr. Bruce. *Soul Guide: Following Jesus as Spiritual Director* (NavPress, 2003).

Doohan, Leonard. *Leisure: A Special Need* (Ave Maria Press, 1990).

Ford, Marcia. *Traditions of the Ancients: Vintage Faith Practices for the 21st Century* (Broadman & Holman Publishers, 2006).

Foster, Richard. *Celebration of Discipline: The Path to Spiritual Growth* (HarperCollins Publishers, 1978).

Foster, Richard. *Prayer: Finding the Heart's True Home* (HarperCollins Publishers, 1992).

George, Christian. *Sacred Travels: Recovering the Ancient Practice of Pilgrimage* (InterVarsity Press, 2006).

Hall, Thelma. *Too Deep For Words: Rediscovering Lectio Divina* (Paulist Press, 1988).

Johnson, Jan. *When The Soul Listens: Finding Rest and Direction in Contemplative Prayer* (NavPress, 1999).

Jones, Tony. *Soul Shaper: Exploring Spirituality and Contemplative Practices in Youth Ministry* (Zondervan, 2003).

Jones, Tony. *The Sacred Way: Spiritual Practices for Everyday Life* (Zondervan, 2004).

Keating, Thomas. *Open Mind, Open Heart: The Contemplative Dimension of the Gospel* (The Continuum International Publishing Group Inc, 1992).

Mulholland, M. Robert, Jr. *Invitation to a Journey: A Road Map for Spiritual Formation* (InterVarsity Press, 1993).

Pennington, M. Basil. *Centering Prayer: Renewing an Ancient Christian Prayer Form* (Doubleday, 1980).

Scorgie, Glen G. *A Little Guide to Christian Spirituality: Three Dimensions of Life with God* (Zondervan, 2007).

Tippett, Krista. *Speaking of Faith: Why Religion Matters—And How to Talk About It* (Penguin Books, 2008).

Willard, Dallas. "How Does the Disciple Live?" (www.dwillard.org).

Willard, Dallas. *Renovation of the Heart: Putting on the Character of Christ* (NavPress, 2002).

Willard, Dallas. *The Spirit of the Disciplines: Understanding How God Changes Lives* (HarperCollins Publishers, 1998).

ABOUT THE AUTHOR

Charles Bello is a writer, pastor to pastors, a trained spiritual director, retreat director, and teacher. He has trained pastors, missionaries and lay leaders in more than fifteen nations. He and his wife, Dianna have six children and live in Edmond, Oklahoma.

Charles is also founder and director of Coaching Saints. Coaching Saints is a small missional community of friends from different church traditions dedicated to calling and equipping Christians to Christ-centered spirituality and Spirit-empowered ministry. This humble band of saints conducts workshops, training events and retreats throughout the world. They love the whole church and are committed to expanding the Kingdom of God whenever and wherever they can.For more information, you can contact them at www.coachingsaints.com.

OTHER BOOKS BY HGM PUBLISHING

PRAYER AS A PLACE:
SPIRITUALITY THAT TRANSFORMS
Charles Bello

Prayer as a Place is an invitation to partner with Christ as he leads the believer into the dark places of his or her own heart. The purpose of this journey is to bring holiness and wholeness to the child of God. With candor and brutal honesty, pastor Charles Bello shares his own reluctance, and then resolve, to follow Christ on this inward journey. In sharing his story, readers gain insight into what their own personal journeys may look like. **Prayer as a Place** reads like a roadmap as it explores the contemporary use of contemplative prayer as a means of following Christ inward.

PASSION FOR THE HEART OF GOD:
MAKING HIS HEART COMPLETELY YOURS
John W. Zumwalt

"Today a revolution is needed; a revolution that needs to take place in the Church, not only in America, but around the world; a revolution that gets people's focus off of themselves and on to God and His glory; a revolution where once again, man will serve God, not God serve man; a revolution that will move the Church to take our Father's glory to all of the nations on the face of the earth. In John's insightful book, *Passion for the Heart of God*, John gives a creative challenge to the Church to pursue God's heart to the ends of the earth. His stories are fresh, energizing and easy to read, but best of all, he holds nothing back. John challenges us all to become a part of the needed revolution. I highly encourage anyone in the Body of Christ to read this book."

— Bob Sjogren, president, UnveilinGLORY and author, *Unveiled at Last*

SIMPLE OBSESSION:
ENJOYING THE TENDER HEART OF GOD
Jamie West Zumwalt

Speaking from her own experiences as a fellow journeyer, Jesus-follower and missionary trainer, Jamie paints an honest picture of her own search for a meaningful, passionate, transformative relationship with God. Her insight into God's desires to be our closest friend, our compassionate father and our tender lover with soften and restore any heart. For all who are struggling or simply going through the motions, these pages will launch you into an exciting new level of reality with Jesus. This guide will show you the way out of unfruitful religious wastelands and into abundant life with your simple obsession.

COMPLETE IN HIM TO COMPLETE THE TASK
James Lee West

"How can we ever hope to have a passion for the lost if there is no passion for Jesus that causes us to leave behind everything that would compete for love and loyalty? The call of Jesus is that we follow Him completely. Unless we are complete in Him, the very idea of completing the commission to go into all the world and make disciples will always remain a mythical part of mere Christian teaching."

— from *Complete in Him*

RECYCLED SPIRITUALITY

$15   SUGGESTED DONATION

Books & resources from HGM Publishing are sold for whatever you can afford.

TO PLACE AN ORDER

Visit the online bookstore   www.heartofgod.com

Call or email Heart of God Ministries   405 - 737 - 9446
                                               resources@heartofgod.com

Or mail the form below to   Heart of God Ministries
                                               ATTN: HGM Publishing
                                               3720 S. Hiwassee Rd.
                                               Choctaw, OK 73020

- -

☐   Please send me _____ copies of *Recycled Spirituality*
        at US $_____ each.
☐   Please send me more information about
        Beautiful Feet Boot Camp missionary training.

Name _____

Address _____

City _____ State _____ Zip Code _____

Country _____ Telephone _____

Email _____

Total Payment Enclosed $_____
                    Please make checks payable to Heart of God Ministries.